Courageous CHRISTIANITY

Bob Moorehead

Eph 5:18

CHRISTIANITY

BOB MOOREHEAD

COLLEGE PRESS PUBLISHING CO., Joplin, Missouri

Library of Congress Catalog Card Number: 90-80686
International Standard Book Number: 0-89900-354-0

Contents

INTRODUCTION

We need a dose of courage! As never before, we need to recover the crispness of courageous Christianity. The Christian life is not just "another way of life," or a "neat movement in which to be involved," or "a good lifestyle to take up" among others. The real thing is a radical thing when stacked against layers of synthetics which we've accumulated through the years. Concerning the kingdom, Jesus said, "violent men take it by force!" (Matt. 11:12, NASB). That's courageous Christianity.

Whatever this movement of Christianity is, you don't just saunter into it casually. It isn't "business as usual." It's not just another issue in life, nor is it an addendum, nor something that's "good for some and not good for all." It's radical, it's life-changing, it's . . . dynamic, to say the least!

These pages were not written out of the conviction that our society is clamoring for the real Christianity of the

5

Bible . . . the fact is, the bulk of our society really doesn't want the return of the real thing. These pages, rather, were written because we have lost, for the most part, the real thing, and it desperately needs to be recovered. The real is buried somewhere beneath the layers of tradition, convenience, selfishness, narcissism, custom, and etiquette.

One day some Greeks came to Phillip, and made a simple request, "Sir, we wish to see Jesus" (John 12:21). They weren't looking for theologies about Jesus, nor were they looking for the eschatology of Jesus, nor did they request an explanation on the organization of this movement, and you won't find where they were searching for messianic scriptures concerning Jesus' pedigree . . . they just wanted to see Jesus, uninterpreted, unvarnished, uncomplicated, unexplained . . . just Jesus.

While our world today would never admit that's what they want, it's certainly what it needs. The problem is that we have drifted so far from the reality and the authentic, every step back is a painful step.

Most of us remember reading in the Old Testament the incident of Hilkiah, the high priest, who found the book of the law in the Temple. A man by the name of Shaphan read from it in the presence of King Josaih. Josiah tore his robes, great conviction came, because the nation had not followed that law, it had been buried and ignored for years. Even when it was read and reread, for the most part, the nation ignored it and treated it as something strange.

That's where we find ourselves today. The real Jesus, the real gospel, the real movement has been covered so long, to uncover it now will present a Christianity to our culture whose demands will seem too harsh, and whose way of life too radical.

Years ago, I heard an evangelist tell of a spring whose waters had certain medicinal properties, so that those who drank from that spring claimed great help with their illnesses.

As time passed, homes were built around that spring, stores went up, streets were cut through, and the day came when visitors asked "Where is the spring from which all this grew?" The red-faced citizens of that town would rub their hands and say, "I'm sorry, but somehow in the midst of our *progress* and improvement we lost the spring and no one knows where it is. No application is really needed, is it? We, too, have lost the well-spring of that vibrant way of life that turned its world upside down, a movement that out-worked, out-prayed, out-gave, and out-lived it's pagan contemporaries.

It's not altogether "safe" to go back to the spring. Our generation of ease, comfort and convenience is not always ready for the real thing to be uncovered, and put back into circulation. If you are totally happy with your level of growth in Christ, if you are content with the state of Christianity in our world today, if you have "bought into" a form of the real thing rather than the real thing, and are content with that, then put this book down, it's not for you . . . then again, maybe it is. On the other hand, if you sense in your spirit that what we're seeing and experiencing today is a far cry from what it was meant to be till the rapture occurs, then read on. But . . . hang on! It took some courage to write some of these things. It will take some courage to read them.

As we seek to "uncover" the real Jesus, who issued the real demands of radical discipleship, and see unadulterated the real way that real lifestyle was lived out, it may be mind-boggling.

There is nothing tame, conventional, or bland about courageous Christianity. As never before it needs to "blow its cover." But like Mt. St. Helens, it will be loud, strong, and the after effects will be noticeable!

1

THE GENUINE JESUS

I was about to "bite." It was the International Market in Honolulu in front of the "Pearl Center" where a large tank contained several oysters that were visible through the clear glass. A young woman had paid the clerk, picked out her oyster, and the clerk was about to remove the little "pearl" embedded beneath the soft tissue. Just as I was debating whether or not to buy a ticket and get a "pearl" a passer-by yelled to the young woman, "not every little silver looking rock that comes out of an oyster is a pearl, lady!" He was right. Only the skillful eye of a certified jeweler with the aid of proper lighting and magnifying glass can tell if one of those "silver rocks" is really a pearl or a nature-made synthetic.

I thought as I walked away ($5 richer) that the same statement can be made about Jesus Christ if slightly rephrased. Not every Jesus that is presented in our world is the genuine Jesus, the one who was born in Bethlehem, grew up in Nazareth, and made the claims he made.

Often today the Jesus presented and preached is "another Jesus." The problem isn't new, however. Paul had to write the Corinthian believers about this problem.

> For if someone comes to you and preaches a Jesus other than the Jesus we preached . . . you put up with it easily enough (II Cor. 11:4).

There is a big move on today in our culture to go back to the basics in foods. People are returning to eating fruit that isn't altered with sugar and additives. It obviously makes for better health, and people are rediscovering a new and fresh taste (really and old taste!) this generation didn't know existed. By the same token, I believe there is a yearning to go back to the original Jesus, and embrace him.

But who is he, and what does he look like and sound like?

Of course he's the son of God, the Messiah, the long awaited deliverer of Israel. Of course he's the one with the Father, and he himself said, "Anyone who has seen me has seen the father" (John 14:9). His real identity is wrapped up in his mission. If we see and understand his mission, we"ll know who the real Jesus is.

HE IS SAVIOR

The angelic messenger made this clear prior to Jesus' birth.

> She will give birth to a son, and you are to give him the name Jesus, because he will save his people from their sins" (Matthew 1:21).

He himself said, "For the son of man came to seek and save

what was lost" (Luke 19:10). His was and is a rescue mission. He did not come to make the world a "better place in which to live." Nor did he come as a social activist to right all social wrongs, and be the champion of straightening out all inequities. Nor was his mission to improve man's moral state, nor did he come to make man smarter, richer, or to give him positive thinking. He came to save, to lift, to do what man, in his sin, could not do . . . to rescue him from himself and from the tyranny of sin that gripped him.

It is interesting, I think, that when the angels announced the birth of Jesus to the shepherds out in the field, they simply said;

> Today in the town of David a savior has been born to you. He is Christ the Lord (Luke 2:11).

Notice: it was not that a "reformer has been born . . . or a king has been born . . . or a conquerer has been born, or a deliverer has been born, (though Jesus was all of those) but a savior.

HE IS A DELIVERER

He not only came to save us from sin, but to deliver us from the bondage sin invariably brings. At the beginning of his ministry, he stood up in the synagogue and said;

> The Spirit of the Lord is upon me, because he has anointed me to preach good news to the poor. He has sent me to proclaim freedom for the prisoners, and recovery of sight to the blind, to release the oppressed, to proclaim the year of the Lord's favor (Luke 4:18,19).

And how he did release. He released men from the grip of demons, from deafness, from blindness, from all kind of disease, fear, and slavery to sin. The Bible says repeatedly that he healed all who came to him.

One of the ways you know if the real Jesus is being presented today is to see if he fits the description of Luke 4. If he does, he's the real Jesus . . . powerful enough to deliver.

HE IS THE LIFE-GIVER

He not only gave the water of life to the woman of Samaria, and Nicodemus, he gives life to all today who come to him by faith. In fact, Jesus himself said,

> I have come that they may have life and have it to the full (John 10:10).

What kind of life did Jesus come to bring? Well, it wasn't just physical life; those to whom he spoke those words already had that. It wasn't just everlasting life; they already had that. Everyone is going to live forever either in heaven or in hell. It was abundant life, a quality of life that is worth continuing on into eternity. He came to turn "existence" into living, drabness into excitement. He came to bring a "zest" to life that can be found in no one else. Someone once said that even if there was no eternal reward in the Christian life they would still be a Christian because of the quality of life enjoyed there. Amen.

HE IS LORD

The word "Lord" appears over 450 times in the New Testament. The Bible talks about every knee bowing and every tongue confessing that Jesus Christ is Lord to the glory of God the Father. The central meaning of that term "Lord" is master, owner, controller, the head. For the believer, there is only one Lord, not several (Eph. 4:5).

In the preaching of Peter on the day of Pentecost, he concluded his sermon with an awesome statement;

. . . God has made this Jesus whom you crucified both Lord and Christ (Acts 2:36).

Christ means the anointed one, but Lord means the supreme one. God made Jesus Lord, and he's Lord, whether you acknowledge him so or not. It's far better to call him Lord and bow the knee now voluntarily, than to do it later involuntarily. Lordship implies surrender and obedience on our part. If we have entered into a relationship with Jesus as our "Lord" we've lost the right to say no to him about anything and also to negotiate with him about anything. His word is final. We don't even have to understand, only obey.

He taught this when he said,

Why do you call me Lord, Lord, and do not do what I say? (Luke 6:46).

Most people have no problem accepting Jesus as the savior of their souls, but they flinch sometimes to accept him as the Lord of their lives. We will see later the heavy implications of Lordship, but for now suffice it to say that as Lord, he holds complete sway over our lives, including all our time, talent, and resources.

HE IS THE DIVIDER OF MEN

That statement may sound negative up front. And there is a tinge of negativism in it I suppose. Because of who Jesus is, the way of life he is, the demands he makes, and the change he makes in our lives, he knew that our embracing him as

Lord would demand some further decisions on our part. Listen to this revolutionary section of the New Testament.

> Do not suppose that I have come to bring peace to the earth. I did not come to bring peace, but a sword. For I have come to turn a man against his father, a daughter against her mother, a daughter-in-law against her mother-in-law, a man's enemies will be those of his own household (Matt. 10:35,36).

On the surface, it sounds like Jesus came to wreck the family. Of course that is not so since he is an advocate of the family. It does say, however, that commitment to him as Lord, allegiance to him as master and owner of all our lives, means division. It's inevitable and can't be avoided. Not all your friends and relatives will be happy because you have sold out to Jesus Christ. The real Jesus presented in the scriptures is one whose met demands will bring division. It goes with the turf, it's part of the package. In the later chapters we will see why, but right now, get it down; His coming brings division. His coming manifests the works of light as opposed to the works of darkness. Lines of division are seen much clearer once we accept him and the way of life he is.

The one thing many Christians fail to see when they become a disciple of Jesus is that their new position will draw fire and friction from friends and family. Many, not prepared for that, desist, and fall back. Courageous Christianity recognizes Jesus as a divider of men. Survivors are those who anticipate the friction that is coming, accept that friction as coming with the territory, and live with it trusting in the Lord for power.

HE IS AUTHORITY

Jesus said, "All authority in heaven and on earth has been given to me (Matt. 28:18). He is the authority over all authorities. We live in a world where respect for authority is taught, but not always obeyed. We respect the authority of the police, the government, the bank, the mayor, the governor, the boss, etc. What we fail to see is that Jesus Christ holds all the authority and the only authority anyone else really has is whatever he is willing to release.

> Everyone must submit himself to the governing authorities, for there is no authority except that which God has established. The authorities that exist have been established by God (Rom. 13:1).

And God has given Jesus all authority, in heaven and on earth. So he is not just *in* government but *above* it. He is not just *in* a political system, he is *over* it. He is Lord of all, not part.

This true identity of the genuine Jesus creates some interesting situations, and changes our whole outlook on culture and society.

HE IS PRESENT

Christianity is the only spiritual religion on earth whose God has opted to live inside the devotee. The Bible makes it abundantly clear that Christ is in us. This is revolutionary to say the least.

> . . . Christ in you, the hope of glory (Col. 1:27).

The real Jesus is not a god who is far away and disinterested in our situation. He is none less than the Holy God, Jehovah who has opted to live, not near us, or above us, or beside us, but *in us*. No one can quite fathom how the holy can live within the unholy, the righteous live within the unrighteous, how deity can live within humanity, but we don't have to fathom the mystery, just accept it and understand the consequences of such a move. His presence makes a big difference on how we indulge our body in sinful pleasure. Since our

15

bodies are called the temple of the Holy Spirit, it makes a big difference what we put into that body, and how we use that body. Thus, Christianity can never be divorced from morality.

The Bible tells us that there is salvation in no one else other than Jesus. Thus he is an exclusive Lord. The Bible also tells us that whoever calls on the name of the Lord will be saved, thus he is an inclusive savior. He is the light of the world, not just another light among lights. He said, "Whoever follows me will never walk in darkness, but will have the light of life" (John 8:12). He is the door through which the sheep pass. There is no other door, in fact by his own words all who came before him were thieves and robbers . . . he's the real shepherd who knows his sheep. He is *the* way, *the* truth, and *the* life, no one comes to God except through him. By his own confession he said to bewildered crowds; "If you do not believe I am the one I claim to be, you will indeed die in your sins" (John 7:24).

He claimed to be *the* bread of life, and promised freedom of hunger to those who come to him; he also claimed to be that water of life that alone quenches the thirst permanently.

HE IS SUPREME

He is the ultimate; ". . . that in everything he might have the supremacy." He is supreme over life, death, marriage, business, fun, pleasure, money, job, retirement, and where does the list stop? His supremacy is confirmed in the last book of the Bible.

> . . . and from Jesus Christ, who is the faithful witness, the firstborn from the dead, and the ruler of the kings of the earth (Rev. 1:5).

King of Kings, Lord of Lords, Jesus is Lord of all!

2

THE BONAFIDE BELIEVER

To say our generation has an identity crisis is a gross understatement! To the government, we're a social security number. To the Internal Revenue Service, we're a tax number. To the telephone company, we're an area code number. To the post office, we're a street address, box number and zip code number. To our creditors, we're an account number. It's no wonder we cringe in the fast food restaurant when upon giving our order, they mechanically say, "You're number 29." Is that all we are? Has our worth been reduced to a digit?

Only a believer in Christ has really become a somebody in a world of nobodies. We have been given a great identity, but unfortunately most Christians don't know who they are or what they have in Christ. It's no wonder many are suffering from an inferiority complex, a low esteem syndrome, a true identity crisis.

It's no wonder that a "rowdiness" has set in. It's no wonder the thrill and excitement is gone for many. They don't know who they are in Christ. Since my esteem is directly related to my position in Christ, I need to be reminded from time to time just who I really am in Him.

YOU ARE A TRUE CHILD OF GOD!

That really doesn't sound very revolutionary, because we live in a world where everyone thinks everyone is a child of God. It's called the "Fatherhood of God and the brotherhood of man." Sounds good, but what the Bible really says is different. Only the person who has accepted Christ as his personal savior is a true child of God in the fullest sense. Listen to what John wrote:

> How great is the love the Father has lavished on us, that we should be called Children of God (I John 3:1).

And that is what we are! That was written by a believer *to* a believer. Only believers have been born again into God's forever family, and only believers can rightfully say they are children of God. Paul said it even more clearly:

> You are all sons of God through faith in Jesus Christ (Gal. 3:26).

It's through faith in Jesus Christ that we're sons of God. Sonship means many things. It means we're related to God, and yes it is a blood relationship. The blood was provided for us when Jesus Christ died on the cross. Sonship also means that God will never turn his back on our relation to Him. If you have a child you cannot biologically "un-child" that person from you. No matter what they do or say, they will be your child. Sonship means we've been given a name, a place, a position in our parent's household. So for starters, if you want to rise above the level of mere mediocrity, know who you are by knowing that you're a child of God by faith in Jesus Christ.

YOU ARE HEIRS OF ALL GOD HAS.

I have never inherited anything from a relative. I understand from those who have, that it is a very exciting thing, especially if the inheritance is sizable in money, lands, stocks, etc. One day you have little or nothing, the next day, you could be a millionaire. That's the way it is when you become a part of the family of God. One day we're without hope and without God, poverty stricken spiritually, and the next day we've come into an inheritance the size of which boggles our highest imagination. Listen to the way the Bible explains it:

> Now if we are children, then we are heirs, heirs with God, and co-heirs with Christ . . . (Rom. 8:17a).

Amazing! That means I'm not only a child of God, but a child that has come into a great inheritance.

Through the great metamorphosis called conversion, we have been changed from a slave of sin to a child of God and have all access to the rights and privileges pertaining thereto. Paul said it again with more crispness:

> So you are no longer a slave, but a son; and since you are a son, God has made you also an heir (Gal. 4:7).

Many Christians live in constant fear that they're going to lose that inheritance before it actually becomes theirs. Peter, however, reminds us that you not only have come into a great inheritance, it is safely guarded by God's power, kept

19

secure until that day!

> Praise be to the God and father of our Lord, Jesus Christ! In his great mercy he has given us new birth into a living hope, through the resurrection of Jesus Christ from the dead, and into an inheritance that can never perish, spoil, or fade, kept in heaven for you, who through faith are shielded by God's power, until the coming of the salvation that is ready to be revealed in the last time (I Pet. 1:3-5).

Wow, what a promise! You ought to feel better already! Your first step out of the blahs has been taken just by believing that you're somebody to God, namely His child and inheritor of all that is His!!!

YOU ARE NOW CLEAN IN GOD'S EYES!!

The devil loves to do a number on believers by reminding them of their past life, and the fact that they still sin, and thus are unworthy in the eyes of God. That puts them on a downer from which most never recover in their feeling.

The church at Corinth was filled with members who had a terrible past. They were former drunks, prostitutes, robbers, liars, plus many other things. Listen to how he explains the great change:

> And this is what some of you were. But you were washed, you were sanctified, you were justified in the name of the Lord, Jesus Christ and by the Spirit of our God (I Cor. 6:11).

Wow . . . what an announcement! Theologians have a word to describe what happened when you got saved. It's the word, *imputed*. It means at the moment of your salvation, all your sin was imputed to Jesus Christ who bore it for you on the cross, and all God's righteousness was imputed to you. Jesus got what He didn't deserve so you could get what you don't deserve. In that sense we can honestly say, "I am righteous." Paul talked about it in terms of "not having a righteousness of my own, that comes from the law, but that which is through faith in Christ, the righteousness that comes from God, and is by faith (Phil. 3:9).

The next time the accuser points his finger at you to accuse of being so sinful, remind him that you have been given the very righteousness of Christ, not because of any of your merits, but because of what Jesus Christ did on the cross.

YOU ARE JUSTIFIED!!

That's who and what you are, Justified. Even before we know what the word means, it sounds good, doesn't it?

> Therefore since we are justified by faith we have peace with God through our Lord, Jesus Christ . . . (Rom. 5:1).

When God saved you, He justified you. Now in our culture to justify means to produce reasons why we're right, but biblically, justify means to make right. God didn't just "declare" us right before Him, he actually made us right. The picture is a courtroom. I'm the defendant. I've been charged with the crime of sin. God is the judge. Jesus is my attorney. He presents my case before the judge and says, "I'll accept whatever penalty is due this person." On that basis, the judge, God, justifies us — he acquits us. Case closed! We have been set free on the basis that the one who had the right to condemn us and sentence us to death (for the soul that sins shall surely die) has reversed his decision and instead, justified us, made us just and holy.

YOU ARE A NEW CREATION

Genuine conversion produces a genuine new creation.

Therefore, if anyone is in Christ, he is a new creation; the old has gone, the new has come (II Cor. 5:17).

Many Christians have bought into a "body-shop" Christianity that teaches that when you come to Christ, you go in and get all the dents straightened, all the scratches touched up, and maybe even a new paint job. Because we get a new nature at conversion, authentic Christianity teaches that we become something we never were before.

I had the privilege of watching two of my granchildren be born. What a miracle. The one thing that really struck me when I saw those new "bundles" of life was, this is a new creation, something that has never existed before. No other person in the history of civilization is like this original.

There are no "duplicates" even with twins. By the same token, when we're "born-again" we become something we never were before, a new creation, a new spirit, a new person altogether.

The best news in II Corinthians 5:17 is that "old things are gone"! Old sin, old ideas, old guilt, old patterns, old problems . . . they're all gone.

What is it that is *new*? We have a new name, we have a new status, we have a new goal, and we have a new family. Courageous Christianity teaches that when we're raised with Christ, we're truly raised to "walk in the newness of life."

WE ARE MARKED PEOPLE!

We talk about a man being a "marked" man, but in real Christianity, it's true. Here's the good news about who we are.

In him, when you believed, you were marked with a seal, the promised Holy Spirit . . . (Eph. 1:13).

Older versions of the Bible use the term "sealed" with the

t, which means the same thing. It is a seal in the se of a state seal, or seal of royalty. We have been sealed, marked, "etched" if you please, with the mark of the Holy Spirit, which Paul goes on to say, is the down payment, or deposit, guaranteeing our inheritance. That means we are secure, our security has God's "mark" on it. Phony Christianity keeps its advocates in suspense all the time, wondering if we're really His or not. What is the implication of our being marked? Basically, it means the mark of ownership, we have been bought with a price, and now belong to a new owner, who has his mark or seal indelibly etched upon us. Praise God.

WE ARE GOD'S SHOWPIECE!

Before you "gulp" on that one listen to what scripture says:

> And God raised us up with Christ and seated us with him in the heavenly realms in Christ Jesus, in order that in the coming ages he might show the incomparable riches of His grace, expressed in His kindness to us in Christ Jesus (Eph. 2:6).

Translated into the vernacular . . . Paul is saying we're God's showpiece, it's in us, the riches of His grace and mercy are perfectly displayed. We are His masterpiece, His workmanship, which He puts on display in the heavenly places for all His creation to see. Far from bringing glory to us, it brings glory to Him.

WE ARE GOD'S RIGHTEOUSNESS

Notice, I didn't say we "have" God's righteousness, though we do, but we *are* His righteousness.

God made him who had no sin to be sin, for us so that in him we might become the righteousness of God (II Cor. 5:21).

No wonder we are His showpiece, it is in us His righteousness is perfectly displayed. You may say, "But there are times when I don't *feel* righteous." True, but thank *God* our position in Christ doesn't depend upon our feelings, but upon the fact of God's word and what it promises. We need to learn to live righteously as we are righteous!

WE ARE RECONCILED

For if when we were God's enemies, we were reconciled to him through the death of His son, how much more, having been reconciled, shall we be saved through His life (Rom. 5:10).

Reconciled implies separation. Prior to conversion, we were alienated from Christ, separated from Him. "Strangers to the covenant" as the Bible says. But because of His love, His sacrificial death on the cross, now that we are saved, we are reconciled, no longer enemies, but friends.

Courageous Christianity teaches us our true identity in Christ. We're not just poor wretched sinners anymore, we've been redeemed, changed, reconciled, made new in every way. Go ahead, enjoy your new identity in Christ, it's part of genuine Christianity!

3

THE REVOLUTIONARY RELATIONSHIP

I was all of ten years old when I joined the club. About five of us boys from the neighborhood found a deserted chicken coop with a tin roof behind Lamar's garage. We made a spur of the moment decision to start a club. We decided it would be called the K-H club since part of us lived on Kirby street and part of us lived on Hurlbert street. What a deep significance to the name! We jumped in, cleaned up the old shack, mixed bags of concrete and poured a floor, painted the walls, bought a lock, posted our sign, then wrote the rules of the club. That last item separated the men from the boys. Because the shack was in Lamar's backyard, and it was Lamar's shed, and Lamar had the keys to the lock, Lamar said, "The only way you can belong to this club is to make me the president and the boss, and anyone, anytime who wants to get in the clubhouse must ask *me* for permission, and that's that!" That really wasn't what the other four of us had in mind — we were thinking more of a democracy where the majority ruled on the basis of meetings and where voting would take place. It was not to be. Lamar spoke with authority, held the keys, spoke the terms of admission, and we could buy in or butt out. We all bought in, on *His* terms. I think the club lasted about thirty days or until summer was over, then it was dissolved. In retrospect, it was a boyhood adventure, just another chapter in the lives of five boys, all of whom are now grown and have grandsons doing the same thing!

I've thought a lot about that chapter in my life — especially in the light of the "Courageous Christianity" into which I bought a number of years ago. It is much like the K-H club in one sense — one man holds the keys, calls the shots, issues the terms, establishes the parameters, and extends the conditions of membership. His name is Jesus.

I had a struggle giving a title to this chapter. I don't want to reduce real, authentic Christianity down to military terms alone, yet let the record read clearly — to become a follower of Jesus Christ demands a relationship with Him that seems revolutionary and radical by the pseudo-standards of 20th century America. We may well have called this section Authentic Priority or "Genuine Joining."

Jesus minced no words, and created no ambiguity when He laid down the terms of our relationship to Him as a believer. When we come to Christ, he gets something and we get something. We get eternal life, the Holy Spirit, forgiveness, and the abundant life. He get us — all of us — those are his terms, and he doesn't water them down or adapt them for anyone. So, look with me at that relationship, and see why it appears to be so revolutionary.

A STRONG LOVE RELATIONSHIP

One of the most misunderstood and misquoted references in all the New Testament is found in Luke 14:26.

26

> If anyone comes to me and does not hate his father, his mother, his wife and children, his brother and sisters, yes, even his own life, he cannot be my disciple (Luke 14:26).

Jesus often spoke in metaphors. He uses metaphorical language here. Now, obviously he was not advocating that we practice hating our relatives, this would have been a violation of the law. Remember, he's talking about our relationship to him in comparison to our relationship to our nearest and dearest. The love and affection we have for him exceeds our love and affection for our own family so much, it makes our love for family to almost seem like hate. It's like driving 55 miles per hour, and a car passes you doing 110 miles per hour. It makes your speed appear to be standing still, but it certainly doesn't mean you're not moving, so don't try to open the door and get out! Jesus is saying that our love and affection for him must exceed that of our nearest family relationships so much, it will appear that we're hating them. This is strong language, yet remember, Jesus was on his way to the cross. His death was imminent. It was not time to play games about the cost involved in following him, no time to be tactful, no time for finesse, he had to make it clear. It's total affection, total love, total loyalty, nothing less will do.

For some to follow Jesus today means family division. It is a high cost to pay. Jesus is saying in verse 26 that if the time ever comes (it has and will in the future) that we must make a decision between love for our nearest loved ones and love for him, there is no question which one we must choose.

Matthew put it in a more positive way when he quotes Jesus as saying,

> Anyone who loves his father or mother more than me is not worthy of me; anyone who loves his son or daughter more than me is not worthy of me (Matt. 10:37).

You can't read that and misunderstand it easily. Jesus drew

the lines of love and loyalty very clearly here. There is no question whatever in regard to where our first affection and dedication ought to be — it's with Jesus, above all else, hands down, no questions asked!

Now in conduct, what exactly does that mean? Why is this relationship considered "courageous Christianity?" Jesus said in Matthew 6:33, "See *first* his kingdom and his righteousness . . . ." Priority is clear. To seek him is to seek his will, his direction, his value system, his ethics, his ways. We live in a culture and have adopted, at least in part, a mindset that says, "don't get too radical or carried away with this Christianity bit, we need a balance, moderation in all things, don't go overboard . . . ." The mindset of a culture that has bought into a cheap imitation of the real thing when it comes to Christianity is constantly making statements like those. This revolutionary relationship with Jesus . . . one that acknowledges him as master, owner, controller, boss, Lord, and supervisor brings about a behavior and a lifestyle that should be so revolutionary, we could easily come off as looking like "fanatics" at the worst or "zealots" at the best. It will change our vocabulary, our outlook, our actions, our relationships, our jobs, our families, our hobbies, our entertainment, our education, our schedules. It will show up on our datebooks and our checkbooks. It will show up in what we read and what we watch. In short, it will make a difference in us. Everything we do, think, plan, and everyplace we go must be passed through the fact that Jesus Christ is Lord, and that we have voluntarily entered into that unique relationship between master and slave.

We used to sing a little chorus:

Not what I wish to be, or where I wish to go,
For who am I that I should choose my way;
The Lord shall choose for me, tis better far I know,
So let Him bid me go . . . or stay.

28

Obedience becomes the order of the day, In fact, the whole Christian life can be reduced to obedience on our part. Jesus made it clear for us with one simple question:

> Why do you call me Lord, Lord, and do not do what I say? (Luke 6:46)

It's as if he was saying, "Obedience goes with Lordship; either obey or quit calling me Lord. I will not tolerate a relationship in name without obedience in practice."

It's no wonder at the close of the sermon on the mount, Jesus gave as a great conclusion the contrast between the man who founded his house upon the sand and the rock. The bottom-line difference in the two men?

> Everyone who hears these words of mine and puts them into practice is like a wise man who built his house upon the rock (Matt. 7:24).

Remember, back in Matthew 7:21, the essence of Jesus' teaching is . . . not everyone who *says* . . . but only he who *does* . . . . The apostle John learned from Jesus well. After the resurrection, after the ascension, he wrote:

> We know that we have come to know him if we obey his commands.

Jesus said; "If you obey my commands you will remain in my love . . ." (John 15:10). Again, "If you love me, you will obey what I command" (John 14:15).

Now, don't misunderstand what is being said here! The Bible does not teach we are saved *by* obedience, but that we are saved *for* obedience. We are saved by God's grace, his free unmerited gift, but once saved, the relationship is to be that of "my utmost for his highest." The word "Lord" is mentioned over 400 times in the New Testament, while the word "Savior" is mentioned only about 24 times. That doesn't mean he's less our savior than our Lord, but it does mean that Jesus went out of the way to describe what that relationship is to be between himself and his followers. It's not a 50-50 partnership, he's not just our "buddy." He's not even our "senior partner." He's our Lord, and we're his slaves. We don't have a say in what he commands us to do, it's not ours to audit it, adapt it, edit it, or even to decide which part of it or how much of it we will do. It's ours only to receive it and obey it.

The great commission ends with; "teaching them to obey everything I have commanded you" (Matt. 28:20). The love relationship we have with Jesus as a disciple, (loving him above all else) demands an obedience. That obedience practically carried out in our lifestyle will cause us to look different from those who have bought into a pseudo-Christianity.

Jesus never hid his scars to win a follower. He never "soft-sold" his claims, his demands, or his expectation. As you read the gospels, especially Luke, you almost get the idea that he discouraged followers from "buying in" too quickly. For example in Luke 9:57-62 we have an account of 3 individual would-be disciples. The first one spontaneously volunteered.

As they were walking along the road, a man said to him, "I will follow you wherever you go." Jesus replied, "Foxes have holes, and birds of the air have nests, but the Son of Man has no place to lay his head" (Luke 9:57).

Notice the man's offer to Jesus; "I will follow you wherever you go." Nothing wrong with a statement like that, it sounds like Jesus has recruited another one. Most of us would have said, "Great, get on board and bring some visitors along with you so we'll have a record attendance today!" Not Jesus. His response is one of cool caution.

I really don't think he was trying to dissuade the man, but Jesus was a realist. Please get the spirit of his response. Foxes and birds are not humans, they're animals. They have lower intelligence, certainly less worth as God measures worth, and are obviously more expendable. Yet even so, they have the security of a home, a place they call home. The Son of Man cannot promise that if you follow him you'll have that luxury. The implication is almost this: "Fine, follow me, but I can't promise you the security of a nice comfortable home and three meals a day — weigh following me carefully — if you're ready for some rough times, come ahead." I hope I'm not putting words in Jesus' mouth, but I really think that is the spirit of the retort.

Right up front, Jesus is honest with the man. Right up front he lets him know it won't be a bed of roses or a piece of cake, in fact it could really get rough before it gets calm.

The second would-be follower is different. He doesn't volunteer, but is "volunteered" by Jesus. Jesus' simple command to this man is, "Follow me" (v. 59). This man responds with a hidden agenda of priorities. He simply said, "Lord, first, let me go and bury my father" (v. 59b). Jesus' response to this sounds cold, terse, and insensitive. "Let the dead bury their own dead, but you go and proclaim the kingdom of God" (v. 60).

Please notice some interesting insights here. First, the man when called to follow Jesus responded with his own set of conditions, his own terms. He wasn't opposed to following Jesus, but was confessing that he would do it on his own terms, "I'll follow you Lord, but *first* . . . ." In other words he established his own priority that would prevail in his relationship to Jesus. Sorry, not permitted! Remember, we come in on his terms or we don't come in at all. Jesus basically tells this man that someone else can do what he was going to do, but for him to do what Jesus told him to do. We don't know whether this man's father was actually dead yet, in the east the term "bury my father" was used to describe the closing time of a person's life, last days of sickness, death, and details of burial; it was also used to describe someone who had already died. In either case, with one sentence, Jesus got this man's priorities back in right order again. On top of that he gave him a command, something specific to do, "proclaim the kingdom of God." This was Jesus' way of saying, "What I'm telling you to do as you become my disciple takes precedence over what you had planned to do." This is truly a revolutionary relationship.

The third man in the trio, like the first, voluntarily offers to follow Jesus: "I'll follow you Lord, *but first* let me go back and say goodby to my family" (v. 61). Oops! Here we go again. This guy is telling Jesus he wants to "buy in" but on his own terms, at his own gait, putting his own interests first. Sorry, it won't work. Jesus' response is too familiar: "No one who puts his hand to the plow and looks back is fit for service in the kingdom of God" (v. 62). Strong words. I mean, what's wrong with an innocent goodby to my family? What harm is there taking a little extra time to go back to the old farm for a family reunion and say goodby officially, I mean, it could be a long time before I get a leave in the service of the Lord. Please note that the issue here is not *what* the guy wanted to do, that in and of itself was certainly innocent. The issue is priority and urgency. If you decide to follow Jesus, do it now, make the break, do it with all the gusto you have, and settle immediately who's going to run the show in your life. It would have been better had this guy said, "I'll follow you Lord, and I would love to go back and say goodby to all the relatives, but I want you to know that's secondary, and I'll do it only if you say it's all right." I think Jesus would have loved to have heard that kind of initial commitment. What he heard was a disciple trying to sneak in on his own terms.

Churches have thousands of people in them today of

these "write-your-own terms" kind of disciple. They abound. If you looked at their date books or calendars, you would find they have been planned for the most part without consulting the one who is supposed to be number one in their lives. A peep into their cancelled checks will tell you immediately whether they've entered the kingdom on the Lord's terms or their own.

It's no wonder Jesus warned in Luke 14 that just as a man who is going to build a tower first sits down and counts the cost, so we must count the cost before jumping on board with him and his cause. Many have signed up for a "compartmentalized" Christianity, where Christ is put on the level of just another compartment of their lives, like their politics, their social life, their occupation, and their hobbies. Not so, he's Lord of all, or not Lord at all. Our relationship with Christ, if we take our cue from Him, is indeed revolutionary when stacked against the "easy believism" so rampant today.

I've found this little self-inventory helpful in developing my own relationship with Jesus. Maybe you will too.

1. Do I desire the presence of Jesus more than any other presence in my life?
2. Does Jesus come first in my daily thoughts?
3. Do I praise Jesus at least three different times a day?
4. Does my financial giving reveal that he's first in my life?
5. Can others tell by my words and actions that I am obsessed with obeying Jesus?
6. Am I virtually free of trying to please myself and instead try to please him in my daily life?
7. Am I willing to be inconvenienced in order to put him first?
8. Would I be willing to sell my home and give all the funds to his cause if I knew he were asking me to do it?
9. Am I willing to put my reputation on the line if putting Jesus first demands it?

10. Am I willing to be involved in some things where it's possible for only him to get the glory?

Think about these things . . . .

4

ORGANIC FRUIT

It is the day of "organic" foods. Everyone seems to want to go back to the basics. It's almost like everyone wants to see on a can of fruit in the grocery store the words, "no additives." No food coloring, no preservatives, no sugar — and we'll all have to admit, there is nothing like that natural taste before it's doctored up with artificial things.

Jesus talked about organic fruit when he gave us another condition of discipleship. Much of the Christianity adopted today is void of the organic. We have rationalized, misinterpreted, skated around the real thing so much that we have read his high and holy demands right out of the scripture. Look at his stern warning:

> This is to my Father's glory, that you bear much fruit, showing yourselves to be my disciple (John 15:8).

There are some things that are obviously clear right on the surface of this verse. First of all, Jesus makes it clear that fruit bearing is to God's glory, not ours. "This is to my Father's glory . . . ." Secondly, he puts the responsibility for fruit bearing directly on us — "*You* bear much fruit . . . ." This isn't a responsibility we can shift to God, it's ours. Then thirdly, he says, *much* fruit! God is the God of much. He wants us to be the same in fruit production. He doesn't want a small crop coming out of us — he's not happy with a "get by" mentality. Then he says, "*showing* yourselves to be my disciples." Older versions of the Bible use "proving yourselves" to be my disciples. The proof, according to Jesus, is in the fruit. It doesn't make much difference in what we say but rather in the presence or the absence of the fruit. Later in that same chapter, he speaks of us bearing fruit that will last, not the kind that will rot, change, decay or blow away when the first wind blows upon it. In fact, he even says that the presence of lasting fruit in our lives is one of the guarantees of answered prayer (John 15:17).

Vital Christianity, the biblical kind, is going to have inherent in it a lifestyle of fruit bearing. The next question is, what did Jesus have in mind here when he talks about fruit? To clear the air, lets make sure what he doesn't mean. In Galatians 5 we are introduced to the fruit of the Spirit. This is character fruit, meaning these are traits believers will have such as love, joy, peace, patience, etc. The John 15 fruit is not character fruit. Character fruit is fruit that we don't produce, it is produced in and through us by the power of the Holy Spirit. That's why it's called the fruit of the Spirit. The whole context of Galatians 5 deals with the work of the Holy Spirit in the believer's life. Nor is Jesus talking about the fruit of righteousness mentioned in Philippians 1:11. There, we are called to be filled with the fruit of righteousness, and this speaks of the fruit that confirms our position in Christ — a position of righteousness. Nor is Jesus talking about the fruit of lips mentioned in Hebrews 13:15:

> Through Jesus, therefore, let us continually offer to God a sacrifice of praise, the fruit of lips that confess his name (Heb. 13:15).

The fruit spoken of here has to do with praise and worship which is the fruit of our lips — or the product of our lips.

The fruit of John 15, I believe, refers to people fruit. We are to be producing people as disciplemakers. Paul once said,

> My dear children, for whom I am again in pains of childbirth until Christ is formed in you . . . (Gal. 4:19).

Paul here saw himself as someone in travail, till he gives birth to people. He saw himself as a producer, not just a consumer. We are in the people production business. Now I realize in the literal sense and technical sense we don't beget spiritual babes, people are born again by the Spirit, but we are in another sense those who produce them . . . we are midwives.

The whole context of John 15 is dealing with the vine and the branches. The lessons are laid out for us clearly. We cannot bear fruit unless we abide in Christ. Jesus said if we abide in him and he in us we will bear much fruit, or people. Someday, I believe God will say to all of us, "Where is your fruit?" In other words, "Where are your people?" We may respond, "What people?" He'll say, "The people you affected for me, the people you brought the message to for me, the people whose value systems you helped shape by my word, the people you trained and affected for my cause and kingdom."

The Bible talks about this in Colossians 1:10 " . . . bearing fruit in every good work," and again in Romans 7 " . . . in order that we may bear fruit to God" (Rom. 7:4).

In Matthew 7 Jesus warned us about the false prophets. He said they would be recognized by their fruit. What was their fruit? Simply producing others like themselves. He went on to say that a good tree cannot bear bad fruit and a bad tree cannot bear good fruit. Then, the punch line; "Every tree that does not bear good fruit is cut down and thrown into the fire. Thus by their fruit you will recognize them" (Matt. 7:19,20).

Courageous Christianity today includes a lifestyle of fruitbearing. Yet so few bear any people fruit to speak of. Only about 3 percent of all believers are involved in bearing fruit that lasts. Since the only thing that will really last is a saved soul that will go on into eternity, it's obvious that Jesus was talking here of people fruit. Today when a person is enthusiastic about sharing Christ with others, he's looked upon as a radical or someone who has gone "overboard" with his Christianity. Yet sharing the good news of Jesus was second nature to the early church. In fact, the apostles Peter and John were commanded to stop preaching and teaching in his name. Their response was, "We cannot but preach and teach what we have experienced." They couldn't help but produce people fruit, it was the natural thing to do. It's interesting, that they were commanded not to, but did, and we're commanded to do it, and we don't.

If this is what real fruit bearing is all about, why isn't more emphasis placed on a lifestyle of sharing Christ? One of the most marked differences in 20th century Christianity and the original pattern of Christianity that we read about in Acts lies just in this area. Somehow, every believer in the first century setting saw himself taking on a lifestyle of a producer rather than a consumer. Consumerism has taken the upper hand in what's passing for biblical Christianity today. How can God bless me? What will the Lord do for *me*? What will happen to me if I give my life to Christ? What's in it for me? How will I benefit? These and other questions abound when people consider "buying in" to the faith today. It was not so in the first century. Christianity was seen, somehow, as an army, the enlistment to which required some output for the enlistee. There was virtually none of the religious professionalism as we see it today. We have so compartmentalized and specialized Christianity today that most think only a few special "professionals" are qualified to produce men for Christ and win other people to Him.

Look at the stark contrast in Acts 8. We are told early in that chapter that a great persecution broke out against the church in Jerusalem, and everybody scattered, *except the apostles*. They didn't scatter for some reason, we really don't know why. Maybe they thought it was better to "hang together than to hang separately." In any event, who scattered? The church members did! These were plain, ordinary, common people like you and me, there wasn't a Bible college trained guy in the bunch, none had been to seminary, none were called "reverends." We would today call them "laymen." They scattered, and Acts 8:4 tells us an amazing thing:

> Those who had been scattered preached the word wherever they went (Acts 8:4).

Who preached the word? The apostles? No, the scattered! Who were the scattered? The common believers. They didn't have to be told to do it, trained to do it, coaxed to do it, begged to do it, intimidated into doing it, they just automatically did it. Why? Because I believe they believed the Christianity into which they had bought was seen as a movement that demanded it. It was part and parcel of the package. It went with the turf!

How different today! In most local churches I've seen, only 3 to 5 percent of the membership is involved in any way as a reproducer of fruit "that lasts." What would happen to the conversion rate in America if we required of every convert to take a vow that sounded like this?

> I,_____, upon my acceptance of Christ, hereby pledge and commit myself to be a fruit-bearer for the rest of my earthly life. I fully understand that bearing fruit means reproducing

in others what someone produced in me, a faith in Christ. I will do all I can to win as many as I can for the rest of my life with the help of the Holy Spirit.

How many would "buy in" if that were a part of the deal? Maybe not as many as are "buying in" now, but wow, what a difference it would make five years from now. I'd rather win ten people to Christ who will be reproducers, than to win 10,000 who will be fruitless for the rest of their lives. This latter method is called addition, when all the time God is calling for multiplication.

Satan's biggest deception, as far as I'm concerned, is the lie that common, everyday folk shouldn't try to take on soul-winning, but leave that to the professionals who are well trained and qualified for it. For about 1800 years, Satan has been fairly successful in peddling that lie. This lie is peddled to you and me in many guises. Here are a few:

1. You better not get involved in something you know nothing about.

It's not how much we know, but how much we care. The old adage is right, "People don't care how much you know till they know how much you care." How true. No, you don't have to know sociology, psychology, or even apologetics. You just have to know what God has done in your life, and be willing to tell others that with enthusiasm. The best witnessing tool today is the personal testimony. The woman of Samaria was hardly a theologian, she wasn't schooled in the humanities or the arts, she just knew that Christ had changed her life, and that's what she went into the village sharing.

2. No one is really interested.

Says who? Admit it, hasn't that thought gone through your mind more than once? It has mine. I've been on the verge many times of saying something to someone else about Christ, when suddenly there flashes through my mind the thought, "They're not going to be interested in this, they're too busy with what they're doing. . . ." Wrong! Our age is convulsing now with a sense of futility. Money hasn't brought happiness and fulfillment, drugs haven't, fame hasn't, nor has fun. Our age is gasping for meaning and fulfillment, and they are, in most cases, ready to listen to anyone who says, "We have the answer." Don't listen to this lie of Satan; it's one of his most effective ones.

3. Rejection is the worst thing.

Satan has convinced many that if people reject your message, it's the worst thing that could possibly happen. Not so. Jesus was rejected more than he was accepted during his earthly ministry. His own home town, and his own race of people did not accept him. In fact, every single disciple that he had affected for over 3 years ended up rejecting him, but it didn't stop him. Nor should it us. If I'm not willing to have the message rejected, I shouldn't be a disciple to start with. Remember, it's not you they're rejecting, it's Him. And even if we are rejected, we ought to thank God that we are counted worthy to suffer for him in that way.

4. My gifts lie in other areas.

This lie has been particularly effective, especially in circles where spiritual gifts are discussed often. Many excuse their non-involvement in bearing fruit, i.e. producing people, by saying their area of giftedness lies in teaching, mercy, or something else. Sorry, but it's not that easy. *Every* believer is called upon to bear people fruit. Not all will have the same results, but all are called to be involved in it.

Witnessing has little to do with giftedness. Jesus said in Acts 1:8 that we all are to be His witness, no one is excepted on the basis of their giftedness. Besides, Isaiah 55 teaches us

41

that God's word will not return empty, but will accomplish what he purposes.

Therefore, another facet of "courageous Christianity" is that it is a fruit-bearing lifestyle, and that fruit is people fruit, not only winning them to Christ, but nurturing them in Christ, and teaching them that they have "bought into" a reproducing movement.

Maybe you're asking by now, "How can I bear more fruit in my life for Christ?" There are some "fruit-fertilizers" that will help you be the kind of fruit bearer God really wants you to be.

1. Daily time in God's word.

Most believers "squeek" by in this area. If you don't believe me, ask five believers you know this question today; "What part of God's word were you in this morning for your quiet time?" Be prepared for them to be a bit embarrassed! I can almost assure you that three or four of them will say they haven't been into the Bible yet today. If you really want God to enable you to bear much fruit, get into God's word, read it, study it, memorize it, hear it, and meditate on it. Spend at least ten minutes each day in memorizing scripture, laying his word up in your heart. There is no short cut to Christian maturity apart from daily time in the word of God. This time should not be for sermon or class preparation, but for personal spiritual development.

2. Spend quality time in prayer daily.

It is impossible to develop a fruit-bearing life apart from fellowship in prayer with the Lord. I don't think God is so concerned with how *long* you pray, but how you pray. Seek his face, spend some time thanking and praising him, spend some more time listening for his voice, spend some more time interceding for others and their needs, spend some more time asking God for wisdom in what he wants you to do. You won't survive long spiritually without a daily prayer time, nor will you ever become a fruit-bearer.

3. Have consistent fellowship with other believers.

Here's a place where you cannot cheat. The Bible is unmistakably clear in its exhortation to assemble ourselves with other believers. It is with them we are strengthened, encouraged, challenged, comforted, and kept fresh. Many think they can miss church and a consistent Bible study and stay strong, not so. Since the fruit God wants you to bear is people fruit, you need to be with people for that to happen.

4. Minister to other people.

Fruit-bearing opportunities arise out of our ministry to others. Unfortunately, many believers have the notion today that God has saved them to sit while others carry the load. This is called "spiritual consumerism" in modern terminology. It's the thinking that we are to be no more than consumers in our Christian walk. The fact is we are not only to consume, but reproduce. It doesn't really matter what your ministry to others is in the body of Christ, the important thing is that you minister with the gifts God has given you.

So, fruit-bearing goes with the package in real Christianity. Without it, Jesus said, we cannot pretend to be his disciples. Half of the battle is won when we realize we are to bear fruit, the other half is won when we're willing to make ourselves available to God. Do it, your life will take on a whole new perspective, and you'll be on your way to living a vital, courageous Christianity!

5

BOTTOM LINE CHRISTIANITY

A company president was doing his best to get all the employees to go into a group health plan. Everyone had signed up except George. They had seminars, film, brochures and still George held out. The president did all he knew to do to convince George that it was a good thing, and how much they needed his participation for the success of the plan. Still, George wouldn't sign. Finally, the president called him into his office and said, "George, we've done all we know to do to get your participation on this health plan, now I want to give it to you straight. Either sign this paper, or you're fired today!" George signed immediately. "I don't understand — all this time and you wouldn't sign, and today, you sign, why?" George responded, "I never heard it put so clearly as you just put it."

I really think that's what the people could have said in Jesus' day when he was through with his discourse in Luke 14.

Listen to the last part of that discourse:

> In the same way, any of you who does not give up everything he has cannot be my disciple (Luke 14:33).

Those are strong words, and in those words, Jesus laid down another condition of discipleship. It's another statement that spells the difference between cultural Christianity and the "courageous Christianity" we read about in the New Testament. I call this bottom line Christianity.

We all know what the accountant refers to as the bottom line. It's that figure at the bottom of the sheet that really matters. Most of us aren't interested in the subtotals; at tax time we want to know what the bottom line says — that's the one that is going to make a difference with us. Jesus, in this verse, laid down the bottom line to his disciples. He established once and for all what his followers' relationship to material things would be if they were serious about following him.

In short he is saying that to be his disciples, we must be committed to management not ownership. Some versions make it even more pointed; they say that whoever does not renounce all that he has cannot be his disciple. The idea here is the bottom line of all Christianity. Jesus is saying, "Get your relationship to things settled or you can never be my disciple." We don't hear much talk about this today. It's not a popular subject. It's not the kind of topic that will attract thousands to a Bible conference, nor do tapes on this topic sell very well.

So, what does Jesus mean by "give up everything he has"? He doesn't mean that to be saved, we must gather up all our money and belongings and turn it over to him or to the church. That may be included later, but that's not his point. Nor does it mean we become a recluse and a hermit, stripping ourselves of all earthly belongings then living off of others.

Jesus is talking about one thing and one thing only. If you're going to follow him, settle up front his definition of your relationship to things, money and material resources.

He's teaching that before we step into his kingdom, before we "buy in" to the movement, we must realize that we don't own a thing. We manage what belongs to another — we manage what belongs to the Lord.

God's ownership of all didn't begin with the teachings of Jesus. It goes way back.

> The earth is the Lord's and everything in it. The world and all who live in it (Psalm 24:1).

I would say that is pretty conclusive, but there's more:

> . . . for every animal of the forest is mine, and the cattle on a thousand hills. I know every bird in the mountains, and the creatures of the field are mine. If I were hungry, I would not tell you, for the world is mine, and all that is in it (Psalm 50:10-12).

As David was motivating people to give to the temple, he said in a prayer to God; "for everything in heaven and earth is yours" (I Chron. 29:11b). In that same prayer, he said, "Everything comes from you, and we have given you only what comes from your hand" (I Chron. 29:14). God owns all, there is nothing outside his ownership.

Jesus made it clear, that to follow him, we must recognize that fact, accept it, confess it, openly acknowledge it, and live it. I hear an expression today that bothers me a bit. It's called the transfer of ownership. I've heard some say, "When you're saved, there must be a transfer of ownership — you transferring to God all that you have." There's only one thing wrong with that teaching; we never owned it to start with. It's pretty hard to transfer ownership from us to someone else when we didn't have it to begin with. A better term is "recognition of ownership."

Jesus once told a parable in Luke 12 about a man who

planted a vineyard, put a wall about it, dug a pit for the winepress, then built a watchtower. He's talking about a land owner who spent his own money creating a grape vineyard. After he made every provision, he rented the vineyard out to some tenants. A tenant isn't an owner, but a manager of what belongs to someone else. In the parable when the owner sent someone to collect the rent and the profits, the renters resented it and threw them out. He kept sending collectors, but they kept rejecting them and killing them.

What a picture of mankind today. God (the owner of this world, his vineyard) has created this place for our enjoyment and puts us over it as managers. He then asks for the rent and what do we do? Usually, man says, "Huh, no way, I've worked hard for what I have, and I'm not going to give any to you." Man begins to think he's the owner instead of a manager. There is a big difference.

Salvation is a free gift, but once we receive it, it costs for the rest of our lives. The biggest cost is just realizing that we really own nothing, we only manage what God has entrusted us to manage. Interestingly, we all manage varying amounts. The Bible teaches in Matthew 25 that the amount depends upon what we have ability to manage. Some have been given much to manage, while others have been given little. The amount really doesn't matter. What matters is to realize that what we manage is not ours but God's.

How, then, does this truth affect our lifestyle? Why did Jesus make this attitude toward things a must if we would be his disciples? People who recognize that God owns all, have several things changed in their life. Look at a few.

ACCUMULATION OF "THINGS" IS NO LONGER NECESSARY

We have become a nation of pack rats. It's called the

adoration of the unpossessed until the acquisition of those things is accomplished. And if we don't have the money to purchase our toys, the plastic card is available to have now and pay later. Boy, do we pay later, in more than one way. The problem in America has become so acute, that in the past fifteen years, we have built thousands of storage buildings where we pay monthly fees to have our "things" stored, simply because we don't have room for them at home.

Jesus made it clear; "A man's life does not consist in the abundance of his possessions"(Luke 12:15). The point is clear. Meaning, significance and purpose are not derived from the acquisition of things. Their presence in no way guarantees success, happiness, contentment, fulfillment or a sense of well-being. We all know that under the hand of a sovereign God, they can all be gone momentarily. Things come and go, Jesus abides forever. This doesn't mean we should not prepare for the future with shrewdness, but it does mean that when you finally accept the fact you don't own something, when it's taken away or lost, you don't feel as though you have lost it, because it wasn't yours to begin with. When I realize I'm just the manager and not the owner, it's no longer up to me to decide how much I'll accumulate, it's up to him.

IT CHANGES MY ATTITUDE TOWARD RELEASING THINGS

There is something wrong with the cultural Christianity into which many have bought when you realize that the average American Christian releases less than 1 percent of his funds for the cause of Christ. This fact reveals that most believers have a struggle in releasing funds. Part of the reason is that they think those funds belong to them. Remember, this was the problem of those men who had been commissioned over the vineyard to till it and keep it. They began to think the land was theirs, that those crops were theirs and that those profits were theirs.

In many churches tithing is taught religiously. Without being harsh on the people who advocate this practice, it does need to be pointed out that tithing was an Old Testament tax imposed on the Hebrews under the law of Moses. It wasn't just 10 percent as most people think. There were actually three tithes Jews were expected to pay. It seems to me that no believer under the New Covenant should do less than tithe 10 percent of his income. However, it's a very poor place to light and stay for the rest of your life. It's a good starting place, but a poor stopping place. Many have been giving the same 10 percent for years, and have never increased in their percentage. In many cases the reason for this is they have a difficult time releasing funds. Why? Could it be they beleive that most of those funds belong to them? I think so.

When you recognize that God not only owns the 10 percent but the 100 percent, you are free to release funds, larger amounts and more often, because it isn't your funds you're releasing, but God's, and he's able to bring them all back so that you can release more! (Luke 6:38).

IT FREES US TO BE RICH TOWARD GOD, NOT RICH IN THINGS

When you buy into the lie that says you own some things, your focus and energies are constantly on material things and how you can acquire more. Jesus told a penetrating parable about a farmer whose crops brought forth plentifully. The harvest was so large, he had nowhere to store them. Isn't it interesting that the farmer's first thought was to *store* the crops? He was surely a man who had not yet learned the principle of management vs. ownership. So, he thought he found a solution. He would tear down his inadequate barns and build larger ones. That tells us much about his thinking. Notice, not one suggestion here about giving away part of his unexpected bounty. So he stored it all up, then said, "Take it easy, soul, eat, drink, be merry." But God called him a fool.

> . . . This very night your life will be demanded from you. Then who will get what you have prepared for yourself? (Luke 12:20).

Jesus went on to say with his teaching that this is how it will be for the person who stores up things for himself but is not rich toward God. Indeed, what shall it profit a man if he gains the whole world, but in the process loses his own soul? It's a poor exchange.

Courageous Christianity places no premium on the acquisition of things, but in fact always recognizes that authentic followers of Jesus acknowledge they own nothing, but can only manage what God has entrusted to them. Paul said in I Timothy 6 that we brought nothing into this world and will take nothing out. That's why you never see hearses pulling U-Hauls. We don't take any of it with us.

See how well you do on this inventory:

1. Am I free from the compulsion to acquire and have?
2. Am I willing to acknowledge that I own nothing?
3. Am I willing to release my home, my car, my savings or anything else when the Owner calls it in?
4. Am I free from a value system that says more is better?
5. Can I honestly be content with what God allows me to manage without coveting more?
6. Am I able to share what I have without reluctance?

I hope you will think about these things.

6

THE WORD TEST

I heard of a Jewelry store near Beverly Hills that had a sign in their window which read; "WE RENT WEDDING BANDS." Don't blame the jeweler! He's simply "cashing in" on a sign of the times. It's called "short term commitments." We see it in marriage, we see it in education, we see it in the field of employment, and where does the list end? It's the age of the "short stint." No one stays at much of anything very long anymore.

Unfortunately, many have bought into that kind of Christianity . . . an "I'll try it and see how it works" kind of experiment. But Jesus said, ". . . he who stands firm to the end will be saved" (Matthew 10:22). He calls people to be long term disciples. Christianity isn't a "Kelly girl" movement . . . where we "occupy" only temporarily. It's a life sign-up.

No wonder, then, Jesus stopped a lot of folk from following him who intended to come on board for the short haul.

If you hold to my teaching, you are really my disciples (John 8:31).

Strong words! That really separates the "men from the boys." Note the condition, "IF YOU HOLD TO MY TEACHING." Some versions say, "If you continue in my word." J.B. Phillips has it, ". . . if you are faithful to what I have said . . . ." Barclay translates it; "If you make my message the FIXED center of your life, you are really my disciples." The New English Bible says it clearly; "If you dwell within the revelation I have brought." The word dwell means here to stay with it, don't bail out.

We live in the age of experientialism; everyone is after an exotic experience of one kind or another. But Jesus teaches us that it's not how high we jump, but how straight and how long we run when we land. Many begin, only a few finish. Blast off is loud and spectacular, it's what all the T.V. cameras cover, it's the event that sends chills up your spine. But all space scientists tell you that blast off is only the gingerbread of the mission. The real test after launch is consistency in space until the final splashdown!

Courageous Christianity, the real kind, goes the distance, perseveres, it hangs in till all the performance is over. Perhaps we've been guilty of not sharing with converts about the permanency of their commitment to Christ. Perhaps we've placed too much emphasis on what God is doing for them instead of what God has called them to do for Him over a lifetime. Someone wisely said that it takes thirty-five years to grow an oak tree, but only three months to mature a squash. But then look at the difference in the material!

I've noticed in over thirty years of pastoring in churches that very few understand the length of commitment they've made to Jesus. As some believers get older, they step aside with the comment, "I've served my time as a teacher, a nursery worker, an usher, or whatever, it's time now to retire and let someone else take over." Where in God's word does that mentality come from? Probably from "Hezekiah 4:12," where all the other fictitious stuff is found.

As you re-read John 8:31, you'll notice what Jesus didn't say; He didn't say, "If you accept my teaching, or if you confess my teaching, or if you endorse my teaching." He said, "If you HOLD to my teaching." He didn't say if you hold to part of my teaching. Nor did he say if you hold to the part that's easy, or the part with which you agree, or the part that's popular and "in." I'm convinced that to "hold" to his teaching is not only hold to it in the sense that you've grasped it, but hold to it in the sense that you won't let it go when adversity comes, or sickness comes, or company comes! You hold to it till death or till Jesus comes which ever occurs first. The question is, "How do we hold to this teaching clear to the end?" Here are the steps, which when followed, should guarantee that John 8:31 will be a reality in your life.

1. FIND OUT WHAT HIS TEACHINGS REALLY ARE

You can't hold to his teachings till you know what they are and where they're found. This demands daily time in the Word, especially in the New Testament, namely in what we call the Sermon on the Mount. That is found in Matthew 5-7 and Luke 6. Even though the teachings of Jesus are scattered throughout the New Testament, they are epitomized in those chapters.

This means you may have to radically change your attitude toward the Bible, and say with the Psalmist, "I love your law." It means you need to thoroughly familiarize yourself with his teaching on forgiveness, mercy, hope, love, service, etc. Unless you are setting aside quality time each day, even if it's only fifteen or thirty minutes to get into God's Word and let its message affect your thinking and your actions, you will never be able to keep his teachings clear to the end. You need to see that time not merely as a neat thing to do, but as an absolute necessity. You need to regard it every bit as important as eating to maintain your physical body. In fact, you need to set a goal to spend as much time nourishing your spirit with the Word of God as you spend nourishing your body with physical food. Quite a challenge!

2. MEMORIZE GOD'S WORD CONSISTENTLY!

The Psalmist said, "I have hidden your word in my heart that I might not sin against you" (Psa. 119:11). There is a direct correlation to "doing the word" and "memorizing the scriptures" that tell us what to do.

My own experience in memorizing scripture has been to memorize large sections and chapters rather than multitudes of disconnected verses on varying subjects. For example, some of the best memorizing to enable you to keep his word all the way to the end is Luke 6, John 15, Romans 12, I Corinthians 13, Galatians 5, Ephesians 4, Philippians 2, Colossians 3, and II Peter 1. The task for any believer is to "walk in the Spirit." The fruit of the Holy Spirit blossoms in our lives when they're drenched with God's Word. Few people will fail to continue with his teachings when those teachings are indelibly "etched" upon his heart, always there for recall when the need arises.

3. BE ACTIVE IN A LOCAL, BIBLE-HONORING CHURCH

True Christianity will always be lived out in relationship to the local body of believers. It is here where fellowship takes place. It is here where accountability is cranked in. It is here corporate worship is experienced. It is here we are constantly exposed to biblical teaching which serves as a reminder to keep his word.

Many have bought into a cheap Christianity that holds aloof from the local body of believers. Remarks like, "I don't believe in organized religion," seek to justify non-involvement. In reality, however, immersion into the local church is a necessity if we're going to stay in touch with those who stay in touch with God's Word. God's church is not superfluous! It's not a "take it or leave it" situation. Jesus established his church for a purpose, and we are central to that purpose, so to side-step that because we have found the church to be imperfect, is to side-step something God calls essential. The Bible says that we ourselves, are the body of Christ, we are the church. Only as our feet are "held to the fire" in a local church setting can we properly mature, and qualify as a true disciple by holding to his word.

4. STAY IN COMMUNICATION WITH GOD BY PRAYER

We desperately need the divine power to keep his word clear to the end . . . that power only comes by a vital prayer life where we're daily coming before the Lord in a time of private prayer. God actually seeks that time with us. He desires that we spend time alone with Him in the prayer closet. Our prayer time needs to be consistent, even when we feel we aren't "getting anything out of it."

Effective prayer-time includes a time to be still before God, a time to worship and praise him, a time to confess our sins and bask in His pardon, a time to pray for others' needs, a time to pray for our own needs, then a time at the end to claim the promise of John 14:13!

I will do whatever you ask in my name so that the Son may bring glory to the Father (John 14:13).

5. SHARE THE TEACHINGS WITH OTHERS

We cannot keep what we will not share. We cannot hold what we will not give away. Unless you are, in some form, sharing Christ and his teachings with others, they will not remain a part of your life. The Bible tells us that the early believers "preached the word wherever they went." As they went, they shared, they talked, they told the good news to others. "Courageous" Christianity gossips the gospel. It is evangelistic at its heart. A lady asked me once if I was one of those "kinds" of Christians that tried to get other people to accept Christ. I assured her I was, to which she responded, "I don't like that brand of Christianity." The truth is, however, that it is precisely that "BRAND" of Christianity that is the real thing. Her brand of "live and let live, and never tell anyone about life" is an invention of the devil, and he's done a fair job of convincing many Christians that that is biblical Christianity. How sad. If you have bought into a "silent" Christianity, you have bought into a cheap imitation of the real thing.

It's interesting to me that in the book of Acts, Peter and John were commanded by the world to stop preaching the message, and they didn't. We are commanded by the Savior TO preach it and we don't! What a paradox. Remember, Jesus never commanded the world to go to church, but he has commanded the church to go to the world. That's us.

6. PRACTICE BIBLICAL STEWARDSHIP

While we've briefly discussed a believer's relationship to "things" and money, yet little has been said about our obligation to give. The subject of "giving" is the most unpopular topic to write or speak about. Yet part of "holding to His word" definitely includes consistent obedience in the area of finances, especially the area of giving.

God never intended that giving be an unpleasant, defeated, dreaded act. On the contrary, he intended that it be a happy, glorious, exciting thing, something that causes us to grow in the grace and knowledge of Jesus. In fact, I believe that unless we get delivered from blindness and superstition in this area, we will never grow significantly.

Jesus said more about a man's relationship to material things than he said about heaven, hell, baptism, judgement and the second coming all put together! If it was important to him in his teaching, then it's important to us if we're going to continue in the word. For starters, Jesus made a significant statement in Luke 6:38:

> Give, and it will be given to you. A good measure pressed down, shaken together, and running over into your lap. For with the measure you use it will be measured to you (Luke 6:38).

That is a revolutionary statement, and concealed in that statement is God's program for financing the work of His kingdom. It is consistent with teaching elsewhere in scripture. It is the principle that says whatever we sow we will reap. In Proverbs 3:9-10 it says:

> Honor the Lord with your wealth, with the firstfruits of all your crops; then your barns will be filled to overflowing, and your vats will brim over with new wine (Prov. 3:9-10).

If you look closely at those verses, you will find there is a command and a promise. Where you see a command and a promise together in the Bible, you better take note; God is trying to say something very significant. (Everything God says is significant!)

The command here isn't hard to see. It's "give." Do it now. Do it first. Don't wait till later, till the crop comes in, till the check comes in, do it now. The promise, predicated on the obedience of the command is this, "*THEN* your barns will be filled to overflowing . . . ." Note the sequence. God didn't say, "Wait till you sell your crops, and your wine, then give me some of the proceed." No, no, it's "give first, then receive." That's God's sequence. In fact, the passage in Luke as well as this proverb teaches us that our giving becomes like a lever that releases God's giving to us! That's why later in Proverbs it says:

> One man gives freely, yet gains even more; another withholds unduly, but comes to poverty (Prov. 11:24).

Wow! What a principle. It's the generous man, the man who releases what he has that gets. It's the man who tightly clenches what he has that experiences poverty. Maybe you're thinking . . . "Are you saying that we give in order to get?" That's exactly what God is saying, BUT . . . you don't get just to keep, but you get so you can give even more, so you can get more, so you can give more, and on and on the process goes, thus you have God's marvelous, UNLIMITED plan of giving.

Paul confirms this principle in II Corinthians 9. Listen to this promise when one sows (gives) first:

> You will be made rich in every way, so that you can be generous on every occasion . . . (II Cor. 9:11).

Isn't that fantastic? What a principle. That's why we should never hesitate to give lavishly and promptly, because it becomes the "seed faith" that triggers God's giving back to us!

So, when you hold to the teachings of Jesus, yes, it includes giving, and giving the way Jesus commanded us to give.

7. FULFILL THE ONE ANOTHER MINISTRY

If you study the teachings of Jesus very long, you become keenly aware that his whole ministry was focused on people. He loved people, had compassion on people, prayed for people, healed people, and wove into his disciples' lives their need to do the same. Perhaps his entire teaching can be summed up in these words:

So in everything, do to others what you would have them do to you . . . (Matt. 7:12).

That's the sum of His teaching with the one another ministry. You might be interested, however to know that the Bible speaks much about "one another." Here is a brief list:

Love One Another . . . . *John 15:17*
Confess Sins to One Another . . . . *James 5:16*
Pray for One Another . . . . *James 5:16*
Forgive One Another . . . . *Ephesians 4:32*
Bear One Another's Burdens . . . . *Galatians 6:2*
Teach & Admonish One Another . . *Colossians 3:16*
Be Subject to One Another . . . . *Ephesians 5:21*
Encourage One Another . . . . *I Thessalonians 5:11*
Serve One Another . . . . *Galatians 5:13*
Rejoice with Each Other . . . . . *I Corinthians 12:26*
Weep with One Another . . . . *Romans 12:15*
Care for One Another . . . . *I Corinthians 12:25*
Depend on One Another . . . . *Romans 12:5*
Be of the Same Mind Toward
    One Another . . . . *Romans 12:16*
Receive One Another . . . . *Romans 15:7*
Show Hospitality to One Another . . . . . . *I Peter 4:9*
Fellowship with One Another . . . . *I John 1:7*

Well, what a challenge! Remember, it's not how fast you get off the launching pad. It's how long you stay in orbit. Many begin, few finish. Be a finisher.

7

THE LOVE TEST

If Martians came in their space-craft, landed on planet earth and began without any help to identify who real Christians were, what would they look for? How would they know? Could they tell by what kind of house they lived in? What kind of car they drove? Could they tell by the personalized license plate that spells JESUS? Or the bumper sticker that says, "honk if you love Jesus"? Or would a better way be to land their craft on Sunday, look for people who drove to church as opposed to those who didn't? What really would be the determining factor?

Jesus really settled the criterion rather simply, yet clearly:

> By this all men will know that you are my disciples, if you love one another (John 13:35).

That's what the Martians would really need to look for. Not

what people said about themselves, not whether or not they could produce an old yellowed baptismal certificate, but . . . do they love? I suppose we really could end the chapter right here because the evidence is all in. The acid test is clearly stated and actually, there doesn't even need to be some kind of scholarly interpretation. If they love, they're real Christians, if they don't, they aren't.

But . . . we have to ask, what KIND of love? Non-Christians have a kind of love, so what makes this love distinctively different? There is quite a gap in what Jesus said and what we actually experience in most Christian communities. As someone so accurately said it;

> To dwell above with Saints we love
> O that will be glory!
> But to live below with those we know,
> Well . . . that's another story!

Love, however, is a big word. In the English speaking world, we have only one word for love . . . it's called . . . love. The Greek language, in which the New Testament was written, has four words for love. However, only two of them appear in the New Testament. A word found in the Greek language, but not in the New Testament is the word *Storge*. It has to do with family ties, our love for things, animals, systems, etc. It can refer to a parent's love for their child, or someone's love for a hobby.

Then, there is *Eros*. This is physical, sensuous love. While not used in the Bible, the principle of sexual love is taught in the Song of Solomon. We get the word "erotic" from this word.

A New Testament word for love is *Philos*, or *Philia*. This is a social love, and is most often identified with the word friend. It is the love of a friend for a friend (John 15:13-14). It is the love of companionship, either in a marriage or in a close friendship.

Finally, there is *Agape* love. This is a divine love, the kind God had when he led us into salvation. It's the love we're called upon to have for one another. This love is uniquely different from anything else or any other kind of human relationship.

If it is the I.D. badge for the believer, the mark by which the world will know we are his disciples, it behooves us to "dissect"that word, and to understand clearly what an *Agape* lifestyle looks like. So, what are the characteristics of that love?

1. IT IS UNCONDITIONAL LOVE

It doesn't love "because of," but "in spite of." It is love given, not on the basis of the worth, the beauty, the attractiveness nor the deserving of the object, but rather it is given regardless of the presence of those qualities. Some parents make the mistake of saying; "You do this and I'll love you" to their children. Those children grow up believing that they have to do something to deserve the love of their parents.

I know a fellow pastor who was fired from his church for no apparent reason at all. Somehow in the ministry there is a "stigma" attached to a preacher who has been fired. I called him long distance to let him know I was sorry and that I still loved him, no matter what the charges were that his leadership was bringing against him. He later told me that of all his preacher friends, I was the only one who called and said, "I love you no matter what." No, I'm not patting myself on the back, just saying that this was once I was able to administer unconditional love, a love whose intensity and genuineness was not dependent on the condition nor the action of the object.

God loved me unconditionally. He loved me while I was still in my sins . . . while I was still "helpless." Nowhere in scripture do we read about God saying to sinners, "Clean up your act. I'm putting you on probation, and if you behave well enough, long enough, I'll love you and save you." No, just the opposite. He loves us while we are still in our sins and he loves us enough not to leave us the way he found us.

Jesus commanded us to love each other as he has loved us (John 15:12). How did he love us? Unconditionally!

Often we love one another with an "until" love. We love another until they disagree with us, until they lie to us, until they talk about us, until they don't take our advice, until they "mess up" or make a moral mistake. Paul said that *nothing* shall separate us from the love of Christ. That isn't an "until" kind of love.

2. IT IS A NON-DEMANDING LOVE

Biblical love, the kind by which others will know we are disciples of Jesus, makes no demands on its objects. It never says, "I will love you, but I do expect this or that of you." One of the descriptions given by Paul of this Agape love, is that it is not self-seeking (I Cor. 13:5).

In helping a couple to be reconciled after almost a year of separation, the woman said to the man in my office, "I'm willing to love you, but if we move back together, here are the things I demand." At this she pulled a piece of paper out of her purse. I asked her for the paper, and when she handed it to me thinking I would read it, I simply crumpled it up and threw it in my trash can. She was first incensed, but as we began to talk of true Christian love making no demands, she acquiesced and realized it would have never worked putting her husband on a tightrope of demands.

3. IT IS A LOVE THAT WAITS

It never operates by the watch or alarm clock. It goes the

distance and practices longsuffering. It doesn't get in a hurry with timetables and deadlines.

An angry father whose son ran away from home was put in touch with the boy by a long distance phone call arranged at my office. Frustrated, angry, with his pride hurt, this father's end of the conversation was; "Of course I love you, but I want you home in three days or there's going to be trouble." Strange love.

I'll call her Betty Lou. She sat flooding my office with tears. Kevin had left her four months ago. He was living in an apartment alone. No immorality, no running around. He just ran. She had been devastated and her question to me was, "How long do I wait?" My response was not what she expected. "How much do you love him?" I knew she loved him dearly, but was getting "antsy." Kevin came to himself within the next month, repented for leaving, returned home and asked her forgiveness. Her thank you note to me a few weeks later said only one thing; "I'm sure glad my love made me wait." I was glad too.

4. IT IS LOVE THAT COVERS A MULTITUDE OF SINS

Terry and Jason were business partners. Cash flow was tight at best that first year. Then it happened. Jason discovered one day while doing the books that over $800 could not be accounted for in the petty cash. He immediately talked to his partner Terry, who shrugged it off. Becoming suspicious, he confronted his partner. The truth was unmasked. Yes, Terry had taken the money. His wife was having a baby and they had no hospitalization. He fully intended to pay it back later and hadn't counted on the fact it would be discovered. He was "had." Jason had every right to prosecute and thought of doing just that. Being a strong believer, however, he decided to put I Peter 4:8 into practical practice.

Above all, love each other deeply, because love covers a multitude of sins (I Peter 4:8).

"Terry, I love you in the Lord. I know you took the money and I'm not going to report it. I want you to pay it back a little each pay period and I do forgive you." Terry melted! The two men embraced and wept together. Jason forfeited what he had every right to do as a businessman and opted instead to do what he didn't have to do, but chose to do. That was to cover Terry's sin with a blanket of love. This is not an attempt to "excuse" sin, nor justify sin, but simply to let the offender know that his action hasn't changed your love for him.

Paul said it well in the love chapter.

It keeps no record of wrongs (I Cor. 13:5).

J.B. Phillips has really captured the true meaning of that verse when he translated it,

It does not keep account of evil or gloat over the wickedness of other people (I Cor. 13:5). (J.B. Phillips translation)

True love doesn't keep score. A marriage counselor once advised a young couple to do a project. Because their problem was always finding fault with each other, he asked each of them to take a shoe box and put a slit in the lid. Every time their mate did something or said something that was bad, they were to say nothing back, just write it down and put it into the box. At the end of the week, they both opened each other's box. In his box she read all her faults written out on all shapes and sizes of paper. In her box, he discovered to his surprise that on each piece of paper were written these words; I love you, I love you, I love you! That melted his heart, because her love had covered his sin and shortcomings.

5. IT IS A POLITE LOVE

I Corinthians 13:5 says that love is not rude. It is, on the contrary, very polite. If love is the I.D. mark for the world to recognize that we are Christians, it must be so transparent as to always come through polite and gentle. In other words, we need to show by our compassion that we truly love, not just say we love. Nowhere is this more needed than in the love relationship between spouses. Many a husband will be extremely polite all day with his boss, his colleagues, his secretary and the waitress, but come home and treat his wife rudely. The kind of love the world will recognize in us must be a polite love. Politeness is the art of saying the right thing at the right time and meaning every word of it. How we need to practice this in our love relationships.

6. IT IS A NON-JEALOUS LOVE

"Love does not envy . . . " (I Cor. 13:4). The King James version says ". . . is not puffed up." It means that love does not puff itself up. The only person that can make you proud and arrogant is yourself. The very next phrase in I Corinthians says "love does not brag." It's no braggart. It doesn't boast about itself. I have learned that jealousy and boastfulness are twins that run together. In Romans 12 Paul begged his Roman readers not to think of themselves more highly than they ought to think. When we do, jealousy sets in, and a false pride that sets us up for a great fall.

I Corinthians 8:1 says; "knowledge puffs up, but love builds up." Any kind of an attitude that causes us to come off as "know-it-alls" or somehow intellectually or morally superior to others, is not true Christian love.

7. IT'S AN "UN-ANGRY" LOVE

That love chapter goes on to say; "it is not easily

69

angered." The Amplified Bible says; "it is not touchy or fretful." The New English Bible says; "not quick to take offense."

Some people have to be handled with "kid gloves" constantly. Folks have to really watch what they say to them or it will be taken in a wrong way. These are people who constantly wear their feelings on their sleeve, and appear to always be defensive, always ready to take up a fight like a cornered animal.

I'm thinking of someone right now in the church, whose feelings were hurt by someone else working in her area of ministry. It came about in the form of quite an innocent remark, however it was at a time when she was low, so she took it in the worst possible way. But true love is not easily provoked. It's right to be provoked about some things. For example, Paul was provoked over idolatry in the city of Athens. The example of Christ, however, is our standard. The Bible says when he was reviled, he didn't revile in return. He didn't strike back at the drop of a hat (I Pet. 2:23). Agape love never seeks revenge, it never looks for a way to "get back." The Bible says that vengeance is God's. It's not our prerogative!

8. IT IS A "FORGETFUL" LOVE

That doesn't mean it forgets to do things, it does mean, according to I Corinthians 13:5 "it keeps no record of wrongs." As we have seen, it forgets to keep score, and is not standing by to say "hurrah" when someone else falls. This trait is closely tied to the fact that it willingly covers a multitude of sins.

I had the privilege of sitting with a couple in a "reconciliation" meeting. He had repented with great remorse over an affair. She had, with some reluctance, agreed to forgive and have him back. She was a mature believer who had read and re-read every scripture in the Bible on forgiveness. In the meeting, with brokenness and tears he took her hand and brokenly said, " Please, please, please forgive me of that affair!" A few seconds passed as I saw her reach our her arms to him and say, "What affair?" No, she hadn't forgotten, but her verbage was delivering a message to him . . . she wasn't filing his mistake away where she could get to it when she needed to retrieve it. It was past for her, gone! Christian love doesn't carry a tape recorder around or a calculator. It doesn't seek to remember wrongs committed.

In verse 7 of I Corinthians 13, Paul puts some finishing touches on by saying: "It always protects, always trusts, always hopes, always perseveres." Agape love is like that.

Courageous Christianity practices that kind of love. The majority of the Christianity we see in our culture is far from that. Are you loving with agape love? Would the Martians be able to tell by the way you love that you are a Christian? Hopefully, yes!

8

THE CROSS TEST

The staff meeting had funneled into one subject . . . we don't have enough space for all the cars and carcasses! Additional services were suggested, the juggling of existing services came up. When a schedule was mentioned, someone said, "If you go with that, your young couples won't come . . . if you go with the other, your middle-aged folk won't come." This same person, who had read all the church growth manuals and had studied greatly on what the barriers to church growth were said this; "If our clientele is going to come, we've got to make it convenient, comfortable, and quick!" I'll never forget the matter-of-factness of the statement.

I wanted to cry out, "Says who?" Have we really bought into a Christianity of convenience, that makes no demands, that requires no sacrifice, that insists on brevity at the expense of thoroughness? I began to think about the Christianity to which Jesus called people in century one.

> And anyone who does not carry his own cross and follow me
> cannot be my disciple (Luke 14:27).

Strong word, indeed, especially if we really understand in our day what it means to carry your own cross. To a Christianity that has catered to casualness and convenience, this condition of discipleship Jesus explicitly lays down comes as a shattering blow!

"People won't put up with the traffic, they won't tolerate having to search for a parking place, they won't abide having to walk nearly a block to get into the building, they won't come back to a poorly ventilated auditorium, or hard pews, or a poor sound system, or an under-staffed nursery, or a service that runs over for more than five minutes, or a message on stewardship . . ." (where does the list end?)

Please don't think this "sarcastic." Of course, we want things as convenient as possible, we want services to run with as much precision as possible, and we don't want to offend people needlessly. But . . . what about Jesus' words concerning a cross? To a generation of "spectator saints" cross carrying is not really too popular. If you held a Bible Conference at a large church in a large city, and advertised the theme was to be how to carry your cross, you could probably meet each evening in the local phone booth with space to spare! This topic isn't pleasant, popular, or plentiful in our day.

I guess before any of us can take or pass the "cross test" we need to know what it means biblically to carry our own cross. When the Roman government carried out a crucifixion, part of the procedure was for the condemned to carry his own cross part or all of the way to the execution place. When he carried his cross through the city, it was tacit admission that the Roman government was correct in the sentence of

74

death imposed on him, that he was, in fact, wrong, and the Roman government was right. It was an open demonstration that he agreed with the harsh penalty, and proved it by carrying his own cross.

So when Jesus enjoined upon us that genuine discipleship demanded us to carry our own cross, it was to be a public display that Jesus was right, and that the disciples were following him to their deaths.

It also meant that just as Jesus carried a cross, and that cross was symbolic of his death, so our cross carrying proves that we are willing to assume the ultimate (death) when we follow him. It means that our option to follow him may indeed result in the ultimate, our death, and the cross is God's way of reminding us of that.

Courageous Christianity has a cross in the middle of it. Jesus promised those who followed him inconvenience, pain, rejection, no recognition, high risk, low benefits, long hours, short lives, and few, if any, strokes. It was not a movement touting "get rich quick." It was not a plea to "discover your destiny" or "realize your potential." It was an invitation to carry a cross. A cross meant pain, degradation, shame, suffering, inconvenience, and usually death. Today, Jesus doesn't necessarily ask us to die, but he does ask us are we willing to die? He doesn't necessarily ask us to do physical suffering for his cause, but he does ask, are we willing to suffer? He doesn't ask us to strip and divest ourselves of all our earthly possessions, but he does want to know we're willing, and that we've settled the issue of ownership and management.

So when we carry a cross, it delivers a message . . . to Jesus Christ and to our contemporaries. It says, in essence, I am committed all the way, whatever it takes, whatever pain, whatever inconvenience, whatever it costs, if it even means death . . . I'm on board, I'm committed.

Thomas Shepherd said it well over two hundred years ago;

Must Jesus bear the cross alone,
and all the world go free?
No, there's a cross for everyone,
and there's a cross for me.

The consecrated cross I'll bear
till death shall set me free;
And then go home, my crown to wear
for there's a crown for me.

Biblical Christianity says that the cross comes with the package; it is part and parcel of the life. It's only in the 20th century "revised agenda" that there is a "crossless" Christianity . . . one that speaks of ease, comfort, convenience, economy, and "do your own thing."

In retrospect, it's no wonder Paul said that the Jews found the cross to be a stumbling block. For years they had lived beneath the tyrannical rule of foreign conquerors. The Persians, the Babylonians, the Greeks and now the Romans . . . all of these had been masters to the Jews, and how they hated the foreign occupation of their holy land. How they dreamed about the coming Messiah who would rule, overthrow the foreign governments, set up the final Jewish reign, and be the mighty deliverer. What did they get? A low-key teacher who taught them to turn the other cheek and go the extra mile. His army numbered a total of twelve, and the gallant end of his life found him on the wrong end of a Roman cross! No wonder they scorned the cross, far from representing victory, success, and prosperity, it stood as the symbol of defeat and failure.

But look at the Gentiles. For them the cross was foolishness. And no wonder! They were trained in reason, wisdom, knowledge, and logic. They could cough up names like Zeno, Thales, Heraclitus, Xenophanes and Plato! These men they knew and honored, but Jesus . . . who was he? A lowly despised Jew, an itinerant preacher with no degrees after his name, no apparent accomplishments to make him famous, just fanatical claims like his one to be equal with God.

The cross was not on the top ten charts then . . . or now. To carry it could mean to commit professional and social suicide. It could mean your standard of living and life-style will come down several notches. It could mean the loss of so called friends. It could mean moving. It could mean crossing uncharted waters, and plowing new ground even in mid-life.

For Polycarp, it meant being burned at the stake. For Dwight L. Moody, it meant leaving the shoe store and preaching the gospel. For Martin Luther King, it meant taking up the cause of the oppressed and the discriminated to be silenced only by that fatal bullet. For Mother Teresa it means getting hands dirty while lifting the poor and diseased. What will it mean for you? Though it may take different forms in different people, a cross-filled life will mean at least the following adventures.

IT WILL MEAN SOME DIVISION

Because cross-carrying is not the "in" thing in our narcissistic culture, you better count on a parting of ways with some if you carry a cross. The fact is, Jesus promised this would be the case;

> Do not suppose I have come to bring peace to the earth. I did not come to bring peace, but a sword. For I have come to turn a man against his father, a daughter against her mother, a daughter-in-law against her mother-in-law, a man's enemies will be those of his own household (Matt. 10:34-36).

His words don't come any stronger than that. A cursory reading of that passage makes Jesus out to be a real family breaker. In the context, however, it's perfectly clear that he's talking about the result of cross bearing. Only two verses later he talks about the necessity of carrying a cross if we're serious about being his disciple. Following Jesus may repel some who said they were our friends. It may even repel some of our nearest and dearest, our blood relatives. Remember, crosses aren't popular!

Let me warn you now, things can get messy when you pick up a cross. What is passing for Christianity today in many quarters allows you to not lose one "friend" or be unpopular with anyone. Courageous Christianity, however, will eventually bring some division.

IT WILL CHANGE THE WAY SOME THINK OF YOU

Jesus made it clear in that same tenth chapter of Matthew;

All men will hate you because of me, but he who stands firm to the end will be saved (Matt. 10:22).

Now I know those aren't good words to "woo" folk into Christianity, but it's better to know what you're getting into right up front than have it "sprung" later.

Not only does cross carrying bring some division, it stirs up anger and even hatred in the lives of some toward you. Cross carriers aren't voted "Man of the Year." They never receive the "Most Liked Employee of the Week" award. An obese person secretly hates a skinny person. A balding person sometimes inwardly loathes the man with a full head of hair. So, an undisciplined, uncommitted, selfish life greatly opposes a cross bearer. Expect it. Jesus said in the sermon on the mount that we are "blessed" when people insult, persecute, and falsely say all kinds of evil against us because of him (Matt. 5:11).

IT WILL BE A LIFE OF GIVING

Cross bearing gives, it doesn't take. We have a generation of "consumers" in the church who think only of what they can "get" for themselves. They want good feeding, and things provided for their children, but few of them want to give. If you bear a cross, there's no place for whining because nobody gave you strokes. There will be no place for complaining because you didn't get your share. It is a life of giving, sharing, compassion, and thinking of others, not yourself. Along the way, others bearing crosses will give to you, and your sustenance will come from the Lord. But don't expect it to be a life of constant receiving, it is a life of giving.

IT CHANGES YOUR IDENTITY

As stated earlier, when the accused and convicted carried a cross through the city streets, it was a silent confession that he agreed with the state, with those in authority. In fact, he was, in a real sense, identifying himself with the one who put the cross on his shoulders.

By the same token, when we carry Jesus' cross and make it our own, we are identifying ourselves with him, and the way of life he is. We no longer "do our own thing." We have melted our identity into him. We're willing to take on a new I.D. We're willing to be called by his name, champion his cause, walk in his sandals, adopt his set of values, be obsessed with his life objective. I hear the phrase, "I've got to have space for me to be me." Guess what? When you decide to be a disciple of Jesus Christ, you lose your old identity, and become his person. The cross you carry gives silent witness to that fact.

It says, "I agree with his person, I accept who he is, I agree with his atoning death, I believe it was valid to wash away my sin. I gladly take the guff, the heat, the pain . . . I gladly identify myself with him, and this very symbol of victory (though it looks like a symbol of defeat)." Henry Lyte was right when he wrote that old hymn;

> Jesus, I my cross have taken, all to leave and follow thee;
>   Destitute, despised, forsaken, thou from hence my all shalt
>   be.
> Perish every fond ambition, all I've sought and hoped and
>   known;
> Yet how rich is my condition, God and heaven are still my
>   own.
>
> Let the world despise and leave me, they have left my Savior
>   too,
> Human hearts and looks deceive me, thou art not like man,
>   untrue;
> And while thou shalt smile upon me, God of wisdom, love
>   and might, foes may hate and friends may shun me,
> Show thy face and all is bright!

Amen! Want to know the difference between a cheap imitation of the real thing and courageous Christianity? Look for a cross, you can't miss it if you would follow him!

9

THE YOKE TEST

For more than eighteen years, I have worn a little gold-plated pin that has mystified about 90% of those who see it. It is a small little bar with two tiny straps hanging at each end. When curiosity has gotten the best of them, they ask, "what is your little pin?" My response is, "It's a yoke." Some get this strange look on their faces, and you can almost read their minds as they're mulling over what exactly is a yoke? I can see they're wondering if I'm talking about an egg "yolk," or if I'm just Swedish and pronounce the word joke, yoke. Others will say, "Oh, I see," when I know good and well they may see, but they still don't understand what I'm really wearing.

After I've given them ample time, I usually add, "You know a yoke, like a yoke between two animals? Well, I'm yoked to Christ." Some have asked what that meant, and my witnessing door is now open to tell them. But . . . what do I tell them? Twentieth century Christianity knows little of what it means to be yoked to Christ. Not only have I never read a sermon on that topic, I've never seen it as a theme at a retreat, seminar or conference. If a cross lies right in the middle of courageous Christianity, then a yoke certainly lies at the foot of that cross.

The yoke is mentioned in only one place in the New Testament, but the ring of its truth is unmistakable there.

> Come to me all you who are weary and burdened, and I will give you rest. Take my yoke upon you and learn from me, for I am gentle and humble in heart, and you will find rest for your souls. For my yoke is easy and my burden is light (Matt. 11:28-30).

I've been in hundreds of meeting and services where I've heard the first part of those verses quoted, "Come to me all you who are weary and burdened . . . " or as the King James says, "all ye who labor and are heavy burdened." It's been used as a text for comfort for the sick, the bereaved, the bereft, the discouraged and the depressed. And . . . it's a good verse. It is an invitation given by the Son of God Himself to anyone and everyone. He doesn't qualify a select group of folk for the invitation, it's for all.

The next phrase is, however, not an invitation, but a command. "Take my yoke upon you . . . ." It's as though Jesus is saying, "I'll give you rest if you need it, and the way I'll give it is by having you yoke up with me." "Take my yoke . . . ." The terms are terms of recruitment and seeming confinement. Let's peel off some more layers, however, and get to the heart of what Jesus is teaching in this "lone ranger" passage.

To be yoked means to be captured. When I slip my neck into the other half of Jesus' yoke, I am acknowledging that I am His . . . I will go where he goes, eat when he eats, turn when he turns, and stop when he stops. I will move in the same direction with him.

To be yoked is to be re-identified. There is a sense in which we lose our old identity when we accept Christ, and take on as our identity his identity. I remember an old farmer in eastern Alabama that yoked two mules together to plow. Their names were Ned and Fred. You just never saw Ned apart from Fred, or Fred apart from Ned, their identity was found only in the other. I think this is what Jesus must have had in mind when he commanded me to "yoke up with him." To follow him means I have no identity apart from him.

To be yoked means to be effective! Ned could never do alone what he and Fred could do together. Now, that isn't exactly true with us and Jesus. Jesus is self-sufficient and self-reliant, and he really doesn't need us, but O how we need him. To pull the load of life without his neck in the other side of the yoke is only to work twice as hard half as long. The paradox of this verse is that Christ offers rest to all by insisting that they take up his burden.

Strange . . . Christ offers rest to the burdened by aking them to share his burden. His solution for those who are weary and exhausted from toil is to offer them the very symbol of toil . . . a yoke!

Many who are heavy laden are looking for someone to say, "Here, lay down your burdens and rest awhile." Jesus does just the opposite . . . he says take upon yourself my yoke, and by yoking up with me, you will find rest from your burdens. So many wallow in their burdens instead of seeking to find a ministry.

I'll call her Erma just to protect her real name. Talk about burdens. A wife and mother of four children, she was suddenly widowed at age 43. With no job skills she moved with three of her four children to the Pacific Northwest from California, her oldest daughter being grown and married. She found a job, but there were never enough funds. One of her children became a drug addict, and met his death in a cruel fashion. After she supported the other two for too long, they finally moved out. She decided that she would not allow her liabilities to imprison her, and she yoked up with Jesus and found enjoyment in serving others and ministering. She lost her life to find it again! You can do the same.

It seems that the symbol of survival in our culture today is the psychiatrist's couch, when Jesus says it ought to be the yoke. It's when we allow Jesus to help us pull our load that rest comes. But yoking up with him does mean we must lose our own personal desires to align up with his. Perhaps that is why you don't see many (or any) people wearing this symbol to describe their Christian faith.

Yoke-wearing may appear on the surface to be confining, imprisoning, and restrictive. It may sound as though to wear a yoke is an abrasive thing. But remember the rest of those verses in Matthew 11. "My yoke is easy and my burden is light." What does that mean? The Greek word for easy here comes from a word that means "well-fitting." In Palestine at this time, ox yokes were custom made to fit the neck. After it was cut out, it was tried on several times, rubbed and smoothed out so it would not chaff the neck of the ox. In all probability, in those days yoke shops had signs that read; "My Yokes Fit Well!" A well-fitting yoke meant maximum work out of the beast. Jesus himself may have well made yokes with his own father. Jesus says to us, "My yoke fits well." Instead of the yoke being a symbol of confinement and enslavement, it is really a symbol of freedom . . . only as we are yoked to Christ are we finally free to do all we were intended to do and become all we were intended to become.

But let's be realistic. Does our narcissistic age really want to buy into a Christianity with a yoke? Not really! It's too restrictive, too confining, too manipulative, too "legalistic" . . . too demeaning. In our "do-your-own-thing" generation, there is no place for yokes. But remember, when you're irreversibly yoked to him, you have a partner that helps pull when the load is heavy, and someone to converse with when the load is light.

I believe our generation has missed the true meaning of being "yoked" to Christ. So many live the Christian life and do exploits for God in their own strength. Really, I should say they "try" to pull it off in their own strength.

Someone has wisely said that God could withdraw the power of his Holy Spirit from the church today, and probably 80% of those churches would not change, because what they've been doing has been the kind of things that could easily be done in the flesh by human strength and ingenuity.

To be yoked to Christ is an admission on our part that we can't pull it off without his part of the pull. That's why he said, "my yoke is easy and my burden is light." He didn't mean by that statement that the Christian life was a piece of cake and easy. To the contrary, in other places he lets us know it's very costly. What he does mean is that the life he demands of us is accompanied by the strength he provides for us. The "weary and the burdened" really refers to those exhausted from trying to carry on the work of God in their own strength and by their own imagination. This means serving Christ as his disciple never becomes a burden, never turns into a hardship or weariness, because Christ's yoke is our yoke.

One last insight about a yoke cannot go unsaid. When I am yoked with Christ I am near him. I fellowship with him, he talks with me, walks with me, teaches me. I draw sustenance and direction from him. When I divest myself of his yoke, I become distant to him and begin to act with a fatal independence. Thus when yoked, I'm in close fellowship, when disengaged, that fellowship becomes distant and cold . . . thus my effectiveness is reduced to zero.

Authentic Christianity fresh from the book of Acts includes a yoke. It's unavoidable, it goes with the turf. It's part and parcel of a courageous Christianity that can affect our world for change. Are you yoked?

10

THE COST-COUNTING TEST

I confess! I like it when a large crowd shows up for church! I love preaching to a "packed house." There's an aura of excitement when both the downstairs and balcony is full, and there's standing room only.

Have you noticed at most major public events, the announcer will, at some point, say, "Today's attendance is _____!" Usually the crowd cheers, whether it's football, baseball, soccer, the opera, or a stock car race! I've been in many churches when the preacher would say, "Today we broke all attendance records with a grand total of _____ !" The audience breaks out in applause. We Americans are enamored with a crowd. Somehow it has come to be the prevailing criterion of a "successful" event. One of the "trade secrets" of preachers on Monday when they're talking to one another is finding out how many the other had in church yesterday.

There is a sense in which crowds may confirm the success of something. If a stadium holds 60,000 and 22,000 show up, the gate receipts may not pay for the circus or the game. But what about Christianity?

Though it's hard to admit, Jesus didn't seem to be all that impressed with crowds. In fact, on several occasions he said things and did things that appeared to thin the crowds instead of build them. He certainly wasn't a crowd pleaser, even though the Bible does say the people heard him gladly.

Returning to Luke 14, we have an interesting statement in verse 25, "Large crowds were traveling with Jesus, and turning to them he said . . . " (Luke 14:25). He said what? What would you and I have said? What do many popular religious leaders say today? What might Jesus have said? Well, he might have said, "Wow, what a crowd today, does anyone have a count yet?" or "Peter, look at all these people, I hope the pollsters are out today, obviously our ratings are going up with this turn out." He might have even said, "Isn't this great, it makes all the obstacles we've encountered seem miniscule, just look at this record attendance today!" But, Jesus said none of those things. Instead he went into some "heavy stuff" concerning people's affection and devotion to him being much greater than they have for their own parents, he went into the cross-bearing teaching, and he also went into the multitudes of would-be followers.

> Suppose one of you wants to build a tower. Will he not first sit down and estimate the cost to see if he has enough money to complete it? For if he lays the foundation, and is not able to finish it, everyone who sees it will ridicule him saying, "This fellow began to build, and was not able to finish" (Luke 14:28-30).

What do we call this teaching? We might title it, *plan before you plunge,* or *estimate before you erect*, or *calculate before you commit*. Some have found fault with these words and they aren't preached much today, because some people believe they contradict coming to Jesus by faith without having all the facts first.

But what Jesus is teaching here is almost too obvious. Just as a tower-builder needs to make sure he has enough price to finish the tower, so the person in the crowd who wants to become a true follower of Jesus needs to make sure he's counting the cost before he signs up. In no way is this a lack of faith, but rather a deep commitment to go the distance, pay the price, take the guff, and be willing up front to stay in the fray until the task is finished. All Jesus is saying is that to see the commitment to the end could get costly, and you better make sure up front you're prepared to pay that cost.

Courageous Christianity is a Christianity that demands a willingness to pay the price, no matter what. Better to calculate the cost up front, then decide to pay it, than to flippantly jump in with both feet and later fizzle on the launching pad or turn to jelly when the battle heats up.

Jesus used a contemporary illustration for his listeners. He used the constructing of a tower. The point was profound. The tower to which he referred was a vineyard tower which was used in virtually all vineyards. From its top guards were placed to detect thieves who roamed the countryside ready to steal the harvest. An unfinished tower was not only a symbol of shame and degradation to the owner of the vineyard, it was a silent invitation for thieves to come and ravish the vineyard.

The vineyard is likened to our lives. A half-built life not only robs the glory from our master, thus bringing a bad name to our cause, it is an obvious invitation to our enemy that our lives are unguarded.

As a small boy, I used drive across Mobile Bay to the little sleepy community of Fairhope, Alabama. Right on the way to beach and picnic area, nestled then under giant, mossed-laced oak trees was a sign I have never forgotten. It was a foundation of a large house, partially enclosed on the first floor with lumber then brown from age and elements. Weeds had all but covered the concrete footing out of which the thickly rusted re-bar came. A dilapidated unpainted fence encircled the long-abandoned project. Every summer when I would go over to go swimming, I would think, they're going to finish that old house. It wasn't until I had graduated from high school many years later that I learned the history of the unfinished house. A man began that project in 1941. He cleared the land, poured the footings, and erected a side and back wall when World War II broke out. He was drafted, served his four years, came home broke, and was never able to finish the project. It became a symbol in that little town. We called it a monument of the uncompleted. Though I haven't been back to that little town for over 35 years now, I wouldn't be a bit surprised if the rotted remains are still there.

That unfinished house is like a lot of unfinished people who, in a moment of high emotion, began to follow Jesus, but made the plunge without first counting the cost. Real courageous Christianity always counts the cost, pays the price, hangs in for the duration, and doesn't look back. It is a stark contrast to the proliferation of easy-believism so rampant today in so many quarters. Western Christianity has been relatively free from persecution, loss, defamation, and martyrdom. That doesn't mean, however, we can buy into a Christianity that doesn't count the cost.

"But," some of you may be saying as you're reading this, "I thought salvation was a free gift!" Let me reassure you, it is, it is! You can't earn that free gift, merit it, or deserve it, it's absolutely free to us, and no amount of work can earn it. But . . . once we receive that free gift, there is a cost, there is a price, there is a sacrifice. What cost Jesus his life cannot come cheap to us. Because we have received that free gift, it will cost us in dollars, in inconvenience, in time, in energy, possibly reputation, and maybe even our life! Jesus is saying to us clearly, "If you're not willing to count the cost, you better not cross over the line." Now I realize those words aren't popular today in a generation that has bought into cheap discipleship. But they are words that must be said.

Jesus' second illustration is just as vivid, if not more.

> Or suppose a king is about to go to war against another king. Will he not first sit down and consider whether he is able with ten thousand men to oppose the one coming against him with twenty thousand? If he is not able, he will send a delegation while the other is still a long way off and will ask for terms of peace (Luke 14:31-33).

The key word here is sacrifice. The king must be willing to make a sacrifice if his own personal resources are insufficient . . . he must be willing to lose the battle if need be.

What a poignant message here. Before we can "go out" to battle, the sacrifice of self must be in place. Victory won't come by struggle, but by surrender. Death to self must precede any life to Jesus. Inspite of what we may hear today about the need for self-esteem, Jesus' whole teaching for us is that we must die to self, especially that self that insists on sitting on the throne in our lives. There is only one throne in our lives, and it cannot be occupied by two people. Jesus brooks no rivals, he tolerates no less than central place, and this means we gladly lay down our "rathers" at his feet.

One day, James and John came to Jesus to ask if they could occupy top, mid-management positions with him in glory. Jesus' immediate response was;

> You don't know what you're asking, Jesus said. Can you drink the cup that I drink or be baptized with the baptism I am baptized with? (Mark 10:38).

In other words, Jesus settled once and for all that there can be no place of privilege without responsibility. Jesus was talking here about his cup and baptism of suffering and sacrifice. If you don't wear the cross, you can't wear the crown.

Courageous Christianity really isn't very crowded. There was no problem having 5000 when Jesus fed the multitudes, but where was that crowd when Jesus was crucified? Jesus loved each individual in the crowd. He was moved to compassion when he saw the crowds, to him they were like sheep without shepherds.

In John 6:66 there is a strange "progress" report:

From this time, many of his disciples turned back and no longer followed him (John 6:66).

Do you know what amazes me about that statement? If you keep reading, you don't find Jesus panicking or saying; "Please don't leave, maybe we can lower the standards to get you to stay." No, he simply let them go, and said to his little corps of the committed, "And are you too wanting to go away?" (John 6:67a, J.B. Phillips Translation). It's almost like Jesus is saying, "Does anybody else want to leave?" He not only didn't hide his scars to win a disciple, he never tried to maintain a crowd by compromising his demands.

When the rich young ruler came to Jesus and heard what it was going to take, he left because he wasn't willing to pay the price. The punch to that incident is that Jesus let him go. He didn't try to woo him back by changing entry requirement, he didn't even try to convince him with ten good reasons why he should join. He just let him go.

No, the success of a movement does not lie in crowds alone. In fact Jesus said the way is narrow and hard and few there are who find it. Many are called, few are chosen. How about you . . . is yours a Christianity of convenience, or have you counted the cost? Have you entered to go the distance? Have you considered the sacrifice? A few have and do. It's that few whom God will use to be His shakers and movers in a world that is about to fall apart.

I want to pray this prayer and mean it;

> I've counted the cost, Lord, considered the loss, assumed my cross, I'm ready to go or stay, wait or leave, walk or run, sit or stand, spend or be spent, live or die, I've counted the cost! Consume me with what consumes you, Lord, burden me with what burdens you, empty me or fill me, strip me or clothe me, lift me or lower me, display me or conceal me, send me or keep me home, increase me or dwarf me, but control me, use me, I stand at your disposal . . . I have counted the cost! Amen.

11

THE MOUTH TEST

Years ago, another man and I entered a health spa to work out and swim. Since we had been there last, the spa had been acquired by a new owner. He had a rather large sign painted over the entire entrance to the building that read: *If the intake exceeds the output, the upkeep will be the downfall!* The message was clear. If you ingest more calories than you burn up, you're fighting a losing battle! Truer words were never spoken.

The same principle holds true in the spiritual realm. If what we intake from Jesus Christ exceeds what we put out for Jesus Christ we've lost the battle, and become little more than obese, waddling, repositories of scriptural and spiritual truth. Like the Dead Sea, with any outlet, our waters will soon stagnate.

Original Christianity possessed an urgency about it we've long since covered with much debris. It had to be shared,

95

told, communicated, proclaimed, given, and shouted from the housetops. We're back to the principle that is the thesis of this book. When a sub-normal Christianity begins to act normal, it appears to be abnormal. We have been subnormal so long in so much, let someone discover from Scripture normalcy, and it does appear to be something very abnormal, and in some cases even weird.

Biblically, we are won to win, told to tell, saved to serve, changed to challenge, redeemed to re-tell. But the Christianity bought into by most has missed that principle, thus stopping the process so that it has to be begun all over again.

So, what is the norm? I think we get a clue from the book of Acts. Peter and John very naturally began preaching the good news that changed their lives. But they weren't preaching long before the authorities moved in;

> Then they called them in again and commanded them not to speak or teach at all in the name of Jesus (Acts 4:18).

That was like pouring gasoline on a fire! Peter and John's immediate response was;

> . . . Judge for yourselves whether it is right in God's sight to obey you rather than God. For we cannot help speaking about what we have seen and heard (Acts 4:19-20).

Commanding them not to talk about Jesus and proclaim him was like saying to the sun, "don't rise today." It was like commanding the mighty Amazon river, "don't flow anymore." It was like commanding weeds in your yard, "don't grow anymore."

They *had* to talk about him, it was as normal as breathing. Unfortunately, somewhere along the way in the spread of Christianity, the unbiblical thinking entered in that said, "only properly trained, ordained, licensed and accredited clergy can share Jesus Christ." So witnessing for and about Jesus trickled to a halt. It's interesting that today, less than 1% of all Christians in our world talk to other people about Jesus Christ with the view of winning them over to him. What a paradox. In the first century, they were commanded not to tell by their enemies, and they told. We're commanded to tell by our Lord, and we don't.

Jesus did not leave us in the dark about this. In Mark, he said,

> If anyone is ashamed of me and my words in this adulterous and sinful generation, the Son of Man will be ashamed of him when he comes in his father's glory with the holy angels (Mark 8:38).

What is this "unashamedness?" Jesus spells it out just a little clearer for us in Matthew 10:32-33:

> Whoever acknowledges me before men I will also acknowledge him before my father who is in heaven. But whoever disowns me before men I will disown him before my father in heaven (Matt. 10:32-33).

So the "mouth test" is really a confessing and acknowledging test. The woman of Samaria certainly passed that test:

> Many of the Samaritans from that town believed in him because of the woman's testimony . . . (John 4:39).

She was unashamed enough to tell other people about it. Biblical Christianity is a testifying movement. It cannot keep still or quiet, it must speak out and bear a witness because of what the Lord has done.

The man healed at the pool of Bethesda passed the mouth test. The scripture says of him:

The man went away and told the Jews it was Jesus who made him well (John 5:15).

Jesus encouraged those he touched to pass the mouth test. Remember the demoniac in the region of the Gerasenes? Jesus brought a remarkable transformation into his life by delivering him from demon possession, and when the man wanted to join Jesus and go with him, he was commanded:

Go home to your family and tell them how much the Lord has done for you . . . (Mark 5:19).

Courageous Christianity, the kind that will make an indelible mark on our culture must be a Christianity of telling.

What is a witness? By definition, it is a person who is obligated to tell what he has seen and heard. Their testimony is crucial to the outcome of the case. How ridiculous it would be for a witness to take the stand, hear the judge say, "now tell us what you saw," then have the witness just respond by saying, "just look at my life, that's witness enough." Yet that is exactly what a lot of believers say; "I really don't say anything about Christ, I think if I live a good life, people will see that life and come to Christ."

I've never known anyone to come to a saving knowledge of Jesus by looking at another person's life. This isn't to say that our lives as believers ought not to be exemplary, but an exemplary life without the spoken confession of Jesus is an empty sham. The fact is, if Christ has really made a difference in our lives, we won't be able to keep it in.

The late Dr. Halford Luccock tells of visiting in a hospital in New Haven, Connecticut, and seeing a man running down the hall with a little piece of paper in his hand on which was written 98.6. He was stopping everyone he could find, and though his shirt was wrinkled from sleeping on the floor, and he needed a shave, he excitedly shouted, "Her fever is down today, her fever is down today." His little girl had lain sick for two weeks with a deadly high fever, and for the first time, it broke, and he had some good news. He shared it with whoever he could get to listen. It seems to me that normal Christianity should be like that. Something radical, something miraculous has happened in our lives, and we ought to be verbally telling others about it.

Here's a little self-inventory we all need to take concerning the "mouth test." How well do you score?

1. Have I told all my relatives about what Christ means to me?
2. When exposed to evil, am I willing to put in a good word for Jesus Christ and stand up to be counted?
3. Do I take advantage of opportunities in restaurants, banks, grocery stores, and other public places to engage people in conversations where I can share my brief testimony?
4. Am I willing to risk being called a fanatic by lovingly turning a conversation toward Jesus?
5. Do I say at least one positive thing about Jesus Christ on a daily basis where I work, where I play, or where I engage in my hobby?

Well, how did you do? Maybe you're saying, how can we verbally share about Jesus so as not to turn everyone off in the process? I think we need to seize opportunities. When I ask a clerk in a store, "How are you today?" and their response is, "O I'm just surviving," I try to answer, "Well, I finally found a way to always do more than survive, I accepted Christ as my savior." Short testimony, but appropriate.

A hospital receptionist last week was having trouble finding a room number, and she blurted out, "I must have been born under the wrong sign, nothing's going right for me today." My response was, "When I got born again from above, the Lord gave me special power to cope with days like you're having." Just a brief witness, but how powerful it can become once the Holy Spirit picks it up and burrows it into the person's life.

Ask yourself, "Am I unashamed to be identified with Jesus?" One of the saddest verses in all the Bible is Matthew 26:56. When Jesus was arrested in the garden, and all of his disciples had the opportunity to take a stand and speak on his behalf, they chose to keep their mouths tightly shut.

. . . then all the disciples deserted him and fled (Matt. 26:56).

They failed the mouth test. One of the greatest differences between a cheap imitation of the real thing and the real thing when it comes to Christianity is this very thing. The belief in our hearts must find its way to our mouth.

That's courageous Christianity.

12

THE DIFFICULT TEST

If you have held on this far in the book, you have obviously noticed that we've been talking about a "brand" of Christianity that is neither popular, plentiful, nor easy. We've been holding in stark contrast the original demands of discipleship against the backdrop of what's passing for Christianity today. No serious student of the scripture would dare deny that what is lived out in most quarters for Christianity today is a far cry from what God intended the way to include in our generation.

Add to this thorough reading of Acts in the New Testament, and the stark contrast becomes even more pronounced.

One cannot read the book of Acts today without realizing that first century Christianity had a dynamo present that is obviously missing today. Perhaps the greatest need of 20th century Christianity is the ministry of recovery. To be sure, first century Christianity was birthed and bred in a different culture, at a different time, with the obvious advantage of the freshness and vitality of the new to its credit. But even so, I believe we have a right to believe and expect that those unique and refreshing marks of that early movement ought to be as fresh and powerful today as they were in A.D. 35.

Years ago, J.B. Phillips said it best:

> . . . for this surely is the church as it was meant to be. It is vigorous and flexible, for these are the days before it ever became fat and short of breath, or muscle bound by over organization. These men did not make acts of faith, they believed; they did not "say their prayers" they really prayed. They did not hold conferences on psychosomatic illnesses, they simply healed the sick.
>
> *The Young Church in Action*, The Macmillian Company, 1956, p. vii

Without technology, the printing press, mass media, or quick transportation, these first century Christian zealots outlived, outloved, outgave and outdied their pagan contemporaries. Without sophistication, clout, accreditation, recognition, or the approval of their culture, they were referred to by their enemies as "men who have turned the world upside down" (Acts 17:6). What was their secret? What were the marks, the definite traits and characteristics that caused their movement to stage the most profound revolution our world has ever known? As you look at these marks, one thing is obvious. Most of them are missing in most quarters of the same movement today.

THE PRESENCE OF A WHOLESOME DOGMATISM

The original church didn't beat around the bush in its proclamation of Christ. It called sin black and judgement sure. It never couched the truth of the gospel in "palatable" language so as to be acceptable to the people. In Peter's preaching, for example, on the day of Pentecost, he minced no words in telling the Jews in Jerusalem that they were guilty of killing the Son of God. Without fear of being called a narrow-minded bigot, he further made a very exclusive claim about Jesus Christ.

> Therefore let all Israel be assured of this: God has made this Jesus, whom you crucified, both Lord and Christ (Acts 2:36).

A convicted crowd responded with "what shall we do?" Again, Peter spoke in specifics, not generalities. "Repent and be baptized every one of you . . ." (Acts 2:38a). The first century church always preached with exclamation points, not question marks.

Without fear of being called narrow, Peter later said,

> Salvation is found in no one else, for there is no other name under heaven given to men by which we must be saved (Acts 4:12).

In our present day of synchronistic compromise, statements like that one would be considered quite unecumenical! In a day when absolutes have become obsolete, it is refreshing to read about a movement who thrived on proclaiming nothing but absolutes.

A HOLY BOLDNESS

You don't read far in Acts before you realize that you're reading about a company of the committed who are extremely bold. For some reason, I am enamored with that tell-tale verse that sums up the thoughts about the religious establishment of the day.

> Now when they saw the boldness of Peter and John and perceived that they were unlearned and untrained in the schools (common men with no educational advantages) they marveled; and they recognized they had been with Jesus (Acts 4:13, Amplified Version).

The New International Version says "unschooled, ordinary men." What was the source of their boldness? Certainly not their clout, nor their education. It was the fact they had been with Jesus.

This boldness enabled them to meet any opposition, any enemy, any roadblock, and be victorious. Later in chapter 4, after they were severely threatened, what was their prayer? Did it go like this? "O Lord, save our hides!" No, it went like this:

> Now Lord, consider their threats and enable your servants to speak your word with great boldness (Acts 4:29).

Unafraid, undaunted, uninhibited, and with unconventional methods, they faced their task with a bravery and courage that stopped Rome, and made Herod turn his head. They would not be turned back by opposition, silenced by threats nor backed down by intimidation.

What a vivid contrast with today's strain of Christianity. Where is the audacious boldness that will turn the head of an unbelieving world and cause them to sit up and take notice that we have been with Jesus!

A SUPERNATURAL POWER

A man once stood at the edge of the great Grand Canyon and said, "Something happened here!" No one can look at first century Christianity and not say the same thing. Something unique happened here! Not only did they proceed with a holy boldness, but with supernatural power as though it was the norm rather than the exception.

A good example of this is seen in the healing of the lame man near the Temple. Peter made it clear to the cripple when he had asked for a handout, that while he couldn't give him money, he could give him something better than money, he could give him what he had, power to be healed.

Later when Peter was speaking to the onlookers after the cripple had been healed, Peter said,

> . . . men of Israel, why does this surprise you? Why do you stare at us as if by our own power or godliness we had made this man walk (Acts 3:12)?

In other words Peter made it perfectly clear that the resources for healing that man weren't from Peter.

> By faith in the name of Jesus, this man whom you see and know was made strong. It is Jesus' name and the faith that comes through him that has given this complete healing to him, as you all can see (Acts 3:16).

You see, the church was born in supernatural power. From its inception, divine power was present. It wasn't put together by a committee, a board, a council, or by human architecture. It came about when the long awaited fullness of the Holy Spirit fell on those 120 in the upper room.

Because it was born and bred in power, it was designed to operate in power. It cannot operate on human power and output any more than a 747 can get off the runway by all the passengers hanging out the windows waving hand fans to get the big plane moving. Yet much of the church today, by its own suaveness and technology, seems to operate . . .not well, but it operates. Someone has half-jokingly said that the Holy Spirit could withdraw himself from most local churches, and nothing much would change. Had the Holy Spirit withdrawn himself from the original church in Acts, the whole operation would have been shut down.

13

WHAT WILL IT TAKE?

If you have read this far, you may be saying, "I see the obvious discrepancy in what is and what ought to be . . . now how is it corrected?" More personally, "What can I do to correct the obvious gap in what Jesus intended and what actually is?"

I read somewhere where a hunter stood at the edge of the woods which were filled with bears. His little boy was there with him, and knew about the presence of these giant creatures of the outdoors. The little boy said to his dad, "I can't go in there, there are big bears in those woods and I'm only a little boy." His father wisely replied, "There are lots of little bears in there too." In other words, "Do what you can."

Maybe you're looking at the state of Christianity today and saying, "It's full of inconsistencies . . . I'm only one person, so what can I do?" The answer to that is, you can do much in every way. I strongly believe there are some measures we as individuals believers can take that will make a definite difference. We can all be a committee of one belonging to the company of the committed, the fellowship of the unashamed, who desire more than anything else in life to be what Christ wants us to be, and do what he wants us to do in this life before we die. What are those measures?

DEEPEN YOUR OWN RELATIONSHIP WITH CHRIST

That's where it all starts. A layman in England went to his pastor years ago to find out what he could do to get revival fires started in that land. His pastor wisely said, "Go home, draw a circle on the floor, kneel in that circle and draw near to God and ask him for revival in England, beginning with you. Don't leave the circle till the fire starts in your heart!" That's still good advice, isn't it? There is a principle in the spiritual realm we are prone to forget. That principle is that we will draw people no closer to Jesus Christ than we are! What a sobering thought. No matter where you are with Christ in fellowship right now, there's room for being closer still. Remember, he doesn't move, we do. Let me suggest that you begin with the basic building block that has already been mentioned, your daily quiet time.

We would all like to believe that most Christians have a daily time alone with God. Wrong. The fact is that only a small minority of believers spend time daily in God's word and God's presence in prayer. If you are already doing this, you can skip this step one, but if not, read on. The Bible tells us that Jesus rose a great while before day, went out to a lonely place where he prayed. If the sinless Son of God felt the need to make it essential, who are we that we can afford to miss this priceless time daily?

A quiet time consists simply of a set time, fifteen minutes, thirty minutes, forty-five minutes, or an hour, whatever fits your schedule best, getting into God's word, meditating on that word, then spending some time in quiteness and prayer. The best time for this is early in the morning before the onslaught of the day is upon you. If you wait till evening, even if you're a night person, you will discover that you're too tired to concentrate.

Another thing I suggest to deepen your relationship with Christ is to set aside one day per month for fasting. Start with fasting for a 24 hour period, for example after dinner one evening, eat nothing and drink nothing but water for 24 consecutive hours. Offer your fast for something in particular, such as something you want to see God accomplish in your life or the life of someone else.

An essential part of deepening your own life is memorizing scripture. Instead of memorizing random passages, memorize a whole chapter. It doesn't really matter at what rate you take to memorize, the important thing is to spend at least ten or fifteen minutes doing it *every day*. The psalmist said, "I have hidden your word in my heart that I might not sin against you" (Psalm 119:11). This is why the Bible urges us to "Let the word of Christ dwell in you richly . . ." (Col. 3:16).

Nothing else you do activity wise to lessen the obvious gap that exists will be effective unless your own spiritual life is constantly going deeper, and you're getting to know the Lord better and better with more intimacy.

SEE YOUR WORLD AS THE LORD SEES IT

Over five billion people inhabit this planet. How does the Lord view all those people? I can tell you his concern isn't how educated they are, what their standard of living may be, or how cultured they are. His concern is expressed in the words of Jesus:

When he saw the crowds he had compassion on them because they were harassed and helpless, like sheep without a shepherd (Matt. 9:36).

I firmly believe that we would see more of the real thing when it comes to Christianity if more of us would make a point to see our world as the Lord views it. That means we must take off our rose colored glasses, and become realists long enough to see the world as it really is, confused, empty, poor, without meaning, without direction, and without hope apart from the Lord. It's then we are moved as the Lord is moved. It's then we are challenged to do something about it. How can I ever forget my trip to Asia. In so many parts of that world, the teeming millions were in sight, groping, struggling to eke out of life a bare existence, how can I ever forget the hollow, empty look in their eyes, and sense the deep longing they had for hope, for warmth, for compassion, for someone who would reach out and simply care.

But you don't have to go to Asia. You just have to drive down your street. Look in your own neighborhoods. you see drug addiction, alcoholism, broken marriages and homes, small children left to fend for themselves till their single parent comes home. You see child abuse, violence, unemployment, sickness, and where does the list stop?

I find myself praying this prayer more often; "Lord, let me see the things you see, and be moved with the things that move you." You don't need to go far to look, but you need to train your eyes to see things as God does.

MAKE A DIFFERENCE IN YOUR OWN SPHERE

No matter who you are, what your education is, nor how old or young you are, you can make a difference where you are, where you work, where you play, where you shop. So often many of us dream of being a great missionary or evangelist with great crowds listening to us. Only a few people are really chosen to do that. God's brigade is made up of only a few generals. The rest of us are the common troops whom God desires to make a difference exactly where we are, daily.

Take honesty and integrity for example. When you're given too much change back from the clerk, what do you do? When something isn't marked in a store and you take it to the cash register, and the cashier says, "how much?" what do you say? Do you tell the price that was marked on the shelf, or do you shave off a dollar or two? We can make a difference by our standard of honesty and integrity. We can also make a difference by our witness. A few years ago, for example, I made a new covenant with God that I would never go into a restaurant and leave without saying something to somebody about my Lord, whether it's the bus boy, the waitress, the cashier, the cook, the manager or whoever. I'll admit that sometimes I forget, but most of the time I remember and God has used that in an incredible way for me to make a difference where I am. You can make that same difference for Christ.

Ask yourself this question: "When the unbelieving world looks at me and my lifestyle, do they see the real picture of Christianity or a cheap imitation of the real thing? And remember, friend, the world is watching, very closely.

BE A CHALLENGER TO OTHER BELIEVERS

Believers need to be stretched for growth, and the best way you can make a difference in this world for Christ is to challenge your fellow believers to go deeper, do more, be more and say more for Christ. We are all affected by the role of others in our lives, especially those people who encouraged us when we were down.

The Hebrews writer said it best:

And let us consider how we may spur one another on toward love and good deeds (Heb. 10:24).

What "challenges" ought we hurl to our fellow saints? How about the challenge to become more involved, the challenge to memorize scripture, the challenge to do soul winning, the challenge to tithe and go beyond, the challenge to use their spiritual gift, the challenge to stretch their faith . . . the list is endless. But a simple challenge isn't enough. We usually don't get what we expect from others, but what we *inspect*. We need to follow up our challenge with a check-up. I believe that in the body of Christ, if saints are properly ministering to other saints, it isn't going to be just in the area of encouraging each other, though that is vital and necessary. It's going to also be in the area of going deeper, longer, higher, to new levels of commitment.

Some call this discipleship. Whatever you call it, we all need to be meeting, formally or informally, with a few people with the idea of stretching them and raising their level of commitment, and urging them to do the same with others.

SET GOALS AND MONITOR THEM IN YOUR OWN LIFE

It's amazing how many people go through life without any goals of any kind. They limp along from day to day, only "reacting" to life instead of acting decisively. The old adage is true, especially in the Christian life, "If you aim at nothing, you will hit it.

I heard about the Arkansas hillbilly that many thought to be a sharp shooter. Tourists driving down the highway one day noticed in several pine trees along the roadway white targets with a bullet hole right in the middle of the bull's eye.

112

Tree after tree, mile after mile. While stopped for coffee, they saw a man in overalls holding a rifle. "Are you the sharp shooter that hit the bull's eye on all those targets?" "Sure am," the man replied. "How in the world did you do it every time?" the couple asked. "Easy, nothing to it, I simply shot the tree, then drew the target!" Well, that's one way to it but not the right way.

If you want to play a vital part in narrowing the gap between New Testament Christianity, and the Christianity popular today, set some goals in your life, and pray for God to give you the wisdom and strength to reach those goals.

Someday Jesus will return to get his glorious bride. It will be his bride he's coming to get, not an imitation of the real thing, not a substitute. I'm giving the rest of my life to making sure that I represent that bride accurately. I never want to "buy into" a cheap facsimile, but the real thing. How about you?

GOD, GIVE US MEN

GOD, give us men . . . ribbed with the steel of your Spirit . . . men who will not flinch when the battle is fierce . . . who won't acquiesce at the bargaining table or compromise in principle; Give us men who won't retreat on the battle field . . . men who won't sell out for lucre or convenience; God, give us men who won't be bought, bartered, or badgered by the enemy . . . men who will go the distance, pay the price, suffer the loss . . . make the sacrifice . . . stand the ground . . . and hold high the torch of conviction in the face of pressure. God, give us men obsessed with principle instead of pleasure; committed to truth instead of ease; give us men true to your word, stripped self-seeking with a yen for security . . . men who will pay the high price of freedom . . . and go any lengths for truth; God give us men delivered from mediocrity, men with vision high, pride low, faith wide, love deep, and patience long . . . men who will dare to march to the drumbeat of a different drummer, men who will not surrender right for a mess of pottage, or run from trials and evade conflict. God, give us men more interested in scars instead of medals, work instead of leisure, challenge instead of easy projects, and in winning instead of trying; Give us men who will die for the eternal, rather than indulging their lives for a moment in time . . . give us men who are fearless in the face of danger, calm in the midst of criticism; Give us men who will pray earnestly, work long, preach clearly, fight bravely, love ridiculously, and wait patiently . . . give us men whose walk is by faith, whose behavior is by principle, whose dreams are God's, and whose direction is forward! Give us men whose strength is equal to the task . . . men who won't fade under the searchlight of the enemy, who won't fear at the shouting of the opposition, who won't bend under the heavy load of responsibility. Lord, give us men willing to be a minority, to stand for an unpopular cause, who can perform without approval and applause, who can stay in the battle without being stroked, thanked, awarded, or promoted. Give us men willing to forfeit personal preference for the higher cause, personal rights for deeper responsibilities, and convenient comfort for consecrated convictions.